Heelaway Your Dog

Obedience Competition Training

CHARLIE WYANT

Photographs by Michael Jones

Cover Photograph:
The winning Midlands Obedience Team at Crufts 1984
Sponsored by Dog World, the Breeders' paper, Ashford, Kent
Photographer: Anne Taylor

CANINE PUBLICATIONS

CANINE PUBLICATIONS
21 Burridge Road, Burridge, Southampton, SO3 7BY
Telephone: (0489) 885112

ISBN 0 906422 07 8

Photoset by
Megaron Typesetting, Bournemouth, Dorset
in 10 on 12 point English Times

Printed in Great Britain by BPCC Wheatons Ltd, Exeter

Contents

Illustrations

ILLUSTRATIONS

In the text

About the Author

Throughout his life the author has always had dogs around him, although originally horses were his first love. He started his working life in hunting, polo and racing stables, and then in an endeavour to further his education, he joined the Household Cavalry. Subsequently he became a stud groom, but the war put a stop to his career and the Royal Artillery (T.A.) claimed his services.

At the end of the hostilities, having moved to the village of Littlebourne in Kent, he joined a brewing company and started a small holding as a part time venture.

During the late fifties he began competing with his dogs at obedience shows, but it was the acquisition of his Alsatian bitch, Mandy (Caroline of Hankley, subsequently to become the first of his four Obedience Champions) that was to eventually change his life again. After winning their first Obedience Certificate with a clear round, Mandy and Charlie quickly became stars, taking them to Crufts in 1962 for the first time, where Charlie has competed in successive years until 1978. It was not long after this that his hobby of dogs became his business, establishing training and boarding kennels, and of course breeding Alsatians under the kennel prefix of 'Heelaway'.

Charlie started the Littlebourne club in 1962 and his fame as a dog handler soon attracted enthusiasts to his club. Under his guidance, club handlers have won approximately 120 Obedience Certificates and produced no less than 13 Obedience Champions. Apart from club members, many other dog handlers in the country have taken instruction from him, and following his training methods have taken their dogs to the top.

One of the author's proudest moments was when the Littlebourne Club won the famous 'Guide Dogs for the Blind' competition. They competed with a team composed entirely of 'Heelaway' bred Alsatians against 83 other teams and took the coveted 'Senior' award, losing only 15 marks out of a total in excess of one thousand.

So far, and surely there are more to come, Charlie Wyant has made four dogs Obedience Champions, the other three being Ob. Ch. Cora of Hankley ('Lois'), Ob. Ch. Heelaway Bestone ('Garnet'), and Ob. Ch. Heelaway Unit ('Unit'). His fame as an instructor and handler has spread throughout the land and beyond. Anyone who has attended any of the many training courses that he has run would acknowledge his great training skill and his born ability to hold an audience spellbound.

In 1980 Charlie had the honour to judge The Obedience Championships in the Crufts ring which he had graced as a handler for many years previously. This added a further distinction to his dog career.

Without the 'Master' as he has been called, Obedience would not have one of its greatest characters. No doubt Charlie will continue to pass on his knowledge of dog training, and this book puts his proven methods in print.

Author's Introduction

Training dogs is a major part of my life and something that has given me a sense of satisfaction. I have always tried to study a dog's reaction to any given set of circumstances so that, when applied to training, I shall know better next time.

When Mandy was a puppy, I had the great fortune to attend one of the training courses held by Sandon Moss. His teaching started me off on the right lines. I then joined the South London Dog Training Club and had the benefit of the late Mrs. Freda Usherwood's advice. It was she who put sufficient polish on our work to enable Mandy and I to work in the top classes. Then came Bill Shackleton's lessons, for whilst teaching other people we all need instruction ourselves, and Bill's advice was invaluable.

It would be fair to say that these three people have had the greatest influence upon the obedience training methods that I have evolved. There are two ladies to whom I owe my thanks. My wife Kath who, when I purchased my first German Shepherd Dog in 1956, suggested that I attend dog training classes. She has always given me her support and took part in the sport for several years. My training and handling companion has, since my early training days, been Bing Bellamy. Apart from her stalwart work as the secretary of the Littlebourne Dog Training Club, she has found time to train four Obedience Champions, one of which 'Tick' I was privileged to work in front of the Blue Peter cameras after they had won Crufts in 1969.

This book has come about as so many of my pupils have asked me to put my ideas into print. Dog training is a subject that I understand, but not being a literary genius, I must thank Beverly Etherington. She attended one of my September courses and took copious shorthand notes, and has spent many hours putting them into book form. I am greatly indebted to her, for without her help, this book would not have been possible.

When training dogs, nobody knows all the answers and I am sure that I shall continue to learn. I hope that you will enjoy training by my methods as much as I have.

Charlie Wyant

1

Dog Training Theory

To be the owner of an obedient dog is something to be proud of. However, this book is written for those who wish to go further, by training their dogs to a standard that will ensure success at Obedience Dog Shows. This kind of competition requires an immediate response from the dog coupled with extreme accuracy, and therefore the method of training has a different approach to that used when training the family pet. The handler must learn and understand the basic aids, teaching the dog in an organised and consistent manner, and allowing him to absorb each part of his training before attempting something more advanced.

A dog's needs are few, for if he is fed, watered, groomed and given regular exercise, his only other request might be a dry comfortable bed. However, in modern society, it is the dog owner's duty to go somewhat further than this. The dog needs to know his place in the house without being either spoilt or cowed. How to behave on public transport, in a car, and in the company of other dogs. All these points should be taught to him, and they take time and patience. Once achieved, the pleasure of owning a dog that loves and respects his owner, cannot be measured in pride of ownership or monetary value. It becomes a love bond between animal and man, very much like the union of a perfect marriage. When this relationship becomes apparent to dog and owner, and not before, they will be sufficiently united to think in terms of competition training. Without the love and understanding for one another, the give and take of teaching will never be acquired.

To fully understand the dog is only one aspect of training. The first thing that must be considered is, do we understand ourselves? Have we the patience and tenacity to get to the top? Is our temperament suited to teaching in a calm and efficient manner without imparting fear, yet are we able to correct the dog when necessary?

The temperament of both handler and dog are, in the final analysis, the only means to success, and the handler must learn to adjust his own mannerisms to suit the nature of the dog that he wishes to train. The basic training aids have to be understood, for in general they apply to all breeds. It is not these aids that will spoil a dog, but it is either the lack of them or their incorrect application that causes the trouble. For instance, are they used too fast or too slow, too hard or too gently, too soon or too late, too loud or too soft? These points must be adjusted to suit the dog, and the prospective dog trainer must realise that an adjustment of methods may be necessary with any two dogs even though they may be from the same litter.

Cultivate in the dog the will to please. This can be done by using a pleasant tone of voice. I call it puppy talk, and it should also be used with the adult dog. Whilst it is permissable to use tit-bits, a pat, a stroke, or a verbal 'Good Boy' should be used in conjunction, and soon one or the other can be dispensed with. To avoid the dog looking for a tit-bit prior to completion of the exercise, allow a gap between the praise and the food. If the dog is the excitable type, be calm and gentle, don't bluster. For the more apprehensive dog, do not move the hands too quickly and any time he appears to be worried, stop training and play with him. Go on to something that he understands and do not attempt to train the other exercise for a few days. Don't fall into the trap of giving too much praise for this is worse than giving insufficient. If overdone, it can cause the dog to forget why he has been praised and little has been achieved. As the dog needs to know when he has done right, he also needs to understand that he has done wrong, and this can be achieved by the use of the opposite to a pleasant tone of voice.

It is a fact of life that there are people whose natural tone of talking is all on one level with no peaks or troughs. Such a person talking can sound very monotonous, but think of the effect upon a dog, already incapable of comprehending the literal meaning of words, who has to try to piece together an association of ideas from a noise that has no distinguishing features. Even without this unfortunate manner of speech, it is essential that a prospective dog handler cultivates a definite difference in voice tones to be used as commands. Just as important is the use of certain letters of the alphabet to make a distinction between the sounds. Some letters lend themselves to emphasis more readily than others, the three commands given in Distant Control and the advanced heelwork positions being good examples. The words 'Down', 'Stand' and 'Sit' each contain three different vowels which when emphasised can help the dog to understand the difference. The word 'Down' is usually delivered in a low forceful tone. With the stand and the sit command, one should be delivered in a mid tone and the other in a higher tone. In all three cases the distinguishing vowel of all three words should have the greatest length of delivery time and the emphasis placed upon it. Whilst the tones are varied it is unnecessary for their range to be outside that normally used by the handler, the exception being the person who talks on one level, but nevertheless the dog will require a definite distinction if he is to learn without confusion.

Many dog training books make quite a point about the difference between requests and orders, but I feel that there is only one real request and that is the word 'Come'. But let's face it all the words used to tell the dog to do something are orders to which we expect implicit obedience without question. Providing that there is a definite distinction in the tone and the part of the word to be emphasised, it matters not how they are referred to, hence all references in this book to the words used are to commands.

A little audaciousness in a young puppy must not be allowed to get out of hand, and a sharp rebuke is generally all that is necessary to bring him to order. This is where the tone of voice has so much effect, for if the dog understands the praising tone, he will soon recognise the tone of rebuke. More drastic action can be taken with the dog that definitely defies his handler, but before physical correction is used, it must be clear that it is a question of defiance and not the lack of understanding. Knowing the difference between these two points is the hallmark of a good handler. I try to take instant action for disobedience, give one or more chances for lapse of memory, and start at the beginning again when the problem is a lack of knowledge. By proceeding in this way a bond of confidence can be established between the dog and his handler. However, correction is not the way to teach. It is easier and a more speedy method to repeat the exercise several times applying all the aids, thus ensuring that the dog cannot go wrong. Correction only causes apprehension, and in the long run it is better to ignore faults and use all the aids next time.

The quick extrovert dog usually makes more mistakes than the more placid type, yet the handler must aim to keep his speed and style whilst acquiring perfection. A happy dog working at a smart pace is a joy to watch, and training sessions have to be of a duration to suit his temperament. It might be that ten minute sessions with a little praise is suitable for this type of dog, when one minute's work, lots of praise, and two minutes' play will suit another. Somewhere between these two extremes is the answer for the dog to be trained, but the handler must be the judge of what is the right approach.

To train a dog that will be happy in his work it is necessary to teach him to play, both at home and away from his familiar surroundings. If the dog will play away from home he is more likely to work away from home. Playing with the dog is an invaluable aid and can be used during, or on completion of, an exercise. I use a knotted rag as a toy as it is easily kept in the pocket, but a ball serves the same purpose. Throw the toy in a joyful manner, letting the dog perform a play retrieve. This will overcome any unpleasant memories of the training session and make him look forward to work next time.

It is also useful to teach a dog a release command so that he knows when training is finished. I use the phrase 'That'll do', but any short phrase will suffice providing that it is always the same and that the dog understands it.

Most aids are easily understood by the dog, and the reasons for their use apparent to the handler. A visit to any dog training school will usually teach the best methods to achieve the desired result, but the knowledge of these methods is not sufficient. The timing of them is one of the most important factors, and the handler needs to have the feel for it. No instructor can impart this to a handler, and it will only come if the pupil is prepared to start slowly and cultivate it. I like to draw the analogy between timing and rhythm. If learning to dance, rhythm can be developed, but it is much better to be born with it. A simple example of bad timing is to first step off, give the dog's name followed by the command 'Heel' and then jerk the lead. It's all the wrong way round. The dog's name gains attention, the command 'Heel' and the movement of the lead come next, followed by stepping off with the left leg. Timing isn't always just a case of getting the aids the right way round, and very often is the difference of a split second when using an aid, be it the voice, the hands, or the lead. Remember that the average human takes approximately 160 paces to the minute, so a dog doesn't have much time during heelwork to decide which way his handler is going. It is a good idea to know what it is like being a dog walked at heel, so try walking at a fast pace beside a person who will execute all the turns without notice. Such an experience will give an indication of what the dog is expected to do.

Dogs are often corrected for handlers' errors, therefore it is no wonder that some lag showing little interest in competition heelwork. My advice is to take time, teaching at a slow pace until both dog and handler have perfected the exercise, then as the dog gains confidence a gradual increase can be made in the speed of the pace.

The schedule for obedience tests states that the dog must be worked on a slack lead. Many handlers make the mistake of training their dog on a lead which is far too slack, thus allowing the dog to make a greater mistake than necessary. For instance, after an about turn the dog is able to go on for a yard or more before he can be corrected, but if the lead is reasonably tight the correction can be made simultaneously with the fault occuring. The difference between a tight and a slack lead need only be a matter of two inches enabling correction to be made by just a turn of the wrist. The lead held and manipulated in this manner obviates the necessity to jerk it or wave the hands around in the effort to do so.

Think of dog training faults as a poison, but remember that the antidote can have a more poisonous effect if overdone. We can use the dog that is loathe to sit as an example. The obvious remedy is to use the three aids to compel him to do so, however, if overdone it can make the dog hand shy. Varying the routine and breaking exercises into component parts can stop the poison developing, which will mean that an antidote is not required. The same applies to working in a dog training class, or at home in exactly the order the schedule dictates. Because tests are usually judged in a similar order, is the very reason why that order should be varied.

Remember that the dog must consider the handler to be the leader of the pack. One way to achieve this is to give the dog his favourite bone or his food, and then take it from him for a few seconds. This must be accomplished without the dog showing any sign of resentment, and if he snaps or growls he must immediately be severely dealt with by a quick shaking combined with vocal displeasure. Once this problem has been mastered the other members of the family have to be able to do the same thing. It is not much fun to own an Obedience Champion if the dog will bite the children of the family when a favourite toy or bone is removed. Some dogs will guard a toy, and if anyone passes too close to it the dog may bite. The trouble is that while this may be funny one day, the next day it becomes a sin, so always be the boss from the start, never letting bad habits develop.

With the family dog, children can cause problems. If the household is of the excitable type with children and friends racing around, it can cause the dog to become over excited. Such excitement can lead to play biting which can get out of hand later. Children teasing dogs is to be avoided. Games such as playing 'catch it if you can' with a glove could in future mean that anything moving will get bitten. Children and adults rushing to answer telephones and door-bells can cause a dog to bark, as the signal of these sounds conveys previous excitement to him.

Understanding the sensitivities of the dog's sound, sight and touch is an important part of dog training, and they are all used when teaching. It is no use calling a dog if he is not paying attention, and this applies to all requests and orders. With the dog's attention to the handler's voice the sensitivity to sound comes into operation. Should loud commands be given, accompanied with a clap of the hands, or should they be soft and quiet? Knowing what is right for the particular dog under training is an art, and unless the sound gains the dog's attention the sensitivity to sight cannot be brought into use.

The dog's eyesight is used to follow signals and aids during training, and the handler must understand all its implications. It is wrong to assume that the dog is as far sighted as a human for this is not so. Certainly he has a greater angle of vision than we have, which means that he doesn't have to turn his head as much as we do to take note of a movement to the side of him. Some dogs' sensitivity to sight is such as to cause them to be distracted, so with all these points in mind the handler must assess carefully the sight of the dog under training.

Sensitivity to touch can be a most important factor. Some dogs will flinch with just the lightest touch of the hand on the back, others taking very little notice of a firm strong hand. For example, to place the learner dog in the sit the handler must know just how much zip to give the lead, and how firm or gentle should be the left hand when placed on his hind quarters. A touch sensitive dog will become hand shy if too much pressure is applied, the opposite type of dog taking very little notice if the pressure is too gentle. Just this simple basic movement will involve the dog's sound, sight and touch sensitivities, and everything that is taught to him will involve at least one of the three. So it must be obvious that to understand just the methods of training is not sufficient on its own, there are many other factors to take into consideration.

The choice of a dog is a matter of personal taste. Many breeds compete at obedience shows and all are capable of a certain amount of success. However, the Alsatian and the Border Collie are the breeds that consistently achieve success at the top. With these breeds, it is my opinion that a greater chance of competition success is likely if a puppy is purchased from a known strain previously proven in the obedience ring. When consideration is given to purchasing a new puppy for training, take time and care. No one can accurately predict the adult nature of any given pup, but known strains should give a guide.

Bear in mind that a dog can live to in excess of 14 years, so when making a choice hereditary defects must be considered. Whilst there are many such defects, the main ones are Progressive Retinal Atrophy (P.R.A.), Hip Dysplasia (H.D.) and Epilepsy. If any of the parents shown on a puppy's pedigree were known to have such faults, then the chances that they will have been passed on is considerable. It doesn't matter how well a dog works or how quickly he learns if he will have to be prematurely retired with a defect.

In my opinion temperament is 80% environment and 20% breeding. I would prefer the odds to be somewhat different, with temperament being purely the result of breeding, so that even poor handlers could not spoil it.

My test of determining which puppy to keep from a litter is to look for the extrovert. This type of puppy will often show himself by picking up an article, running around with it and swanking a little. This is usually the right one for work, but it doesn't mean that the retrieve will not have to be taught; it just shows that the temperament is as near perfect as is likely.

2

Deportment

A major obstacle to good dog training is the handler's clumsy body which can be all arms and legs without co-ordination. The damage that can be done by a beginner handler is almost irreparable, and before attempting to confuse a poor little pup it makes good sense to perfect deportment. Remember, for better or for worse, the puppy learns from his handler, and therefore the approach should be careful and confident.

Practising footwork without a dog will inevitably produce some raised eyebrows. However, the handler must be able to walk in such a manner that the correct movement of the feet become automatic, enabling complete attention to be given to the dog. Every movement of the body, especially the feet and hands are an aid to the dog, and a moment's hesitation or a wrong gesture can cost valuable marks in the showring. The rhythm of the walk and the timing only come with experience, so practise walking in straight lines and in left hand circles. Before setting off straighten the body, hold the head high, then crook the left arm slightly as if holding a lead, and swing the right arm in co-ordination with the left leg. Commence footwork practise by taking reasonably short springy steps, then swank a little imagining that you have a Crufts winner lovingly curled to your left leg.

Once the dog handling walk can be changed to at will, and before attempting to train the dog for heelwork, it is advantageous for a friend or fellow club member to call commands, thereby acting as a steward. There is a big difference between practising the walk and footwork on your own and being given commands, and even if late instructions are given or if caught on the wrong leg, the handler must be able to continue smoothly. Always remember that nothing must interfere with the forward impulsion of dog and handler, and if it does the dog is at a disadvantage.

When heelwork is first attempted with the dog, there will undoubtedly be moments when the handler falls over him, finding the lead wrapped round the legs. In such a situation, pick yourself up, relax and try again. If the dog is trodden on accidently, apprehension of heelwork is less likely if soft shoes are worn. However, if he squeals giving the impression that he is being murdered, rather than make a fuss of him, ignore it by assuming the attitude that it is his fault for getting in the way. Such inaction by the handler may avoid the dog becoming one that makes a fuss about nothing.

No matter how proficient the dogless footwork has become, the real thing will not be easy at first. Try very hard not to bend over to look at the dog, especially when turning, and be aware of the temptations of bending forward which often has the effect of making the dog work wide. In such a situation checking the dog in close will only make him apprehensive to the point of working wider, so keep the body upright, the behind tucked in, and turning the head slightly just glance down over the left arm. It sounds difficult but it can be done.

There are correct foot movements for teaching the dog turns from stationary positions and they must also be perfected before the dog is subjected to clumsy handling. Every such turn should be finished by placing the dog in the sit position and there is a right way for this simple move to be performed. With the dog standing at heel, shorten the lead a little and transfer it to the right hand. Raise this hand above and behind the dog's head and press lightly on his backside with the left hand, simultaneously giving the command 'Sit'. These movements are referred to as 'the three aids', and even when the dog knows the exercise they should be used frequently. I make no apology for continually referring to them in this book, as they are so important. They ensure that the dog always obeys the command, that the exercise is executed immediately, and that he sits close and straight. When given the command to sit it is likely that a puppy will swing round to look at the handler, usually in anticipation of a tit-bit. So when giving the second aid guide the puppy's bottom down to your heel using the left hand to do so. If this is always done he will not know any other way and the golden rule will be fulfilled, 'don't correct, never let it happen in the first place'.

At all times when moving forward together the handler should commence by moving the left leg, and by carefully exaggerating the footwork, a pup can be taught which leg to follow. At any time when leaving the dog, step off with the right leg moving slightly to the right, giving a pronounced hand signal to the dog which will mean 'Wait', or 'Stay'. Thus additional signals are being given to help the dog to know what the handler intends. When coming to a halt, try to keep the shoulders straight and halt so that the left leg makes the final movement. I call this halt 'left leg up to right', and although it should never have been allowed to develop in the first place, if the dog has learned to sit forward, halt with the right leg coming up to the left.

To stop the dog crabbing or forward working, some handlers drop the left shoulder, a posture which is sometimes good-naturedly referred to as 'Collie Cramp'. This term has been evolved from the rather uncomfortable way some Border Collie handlers endeavour to keep their dog back, and if possible it should be avoided. There are dogs that are oversensitive to shoulder movements and it may be found that heelwork becomes impossible because of the effort to maintain them, and in the show ring unnecessary body movement is penalised, so don't start it. If the dog sits slightly back from the correct position, try halting with the left leg up to the right, and if the problem is very bad turn the left toe slightly towards the right foot. This should bring the dog forward in anticipation of a right turn. However, if a judge spots such a move marks will be lost. Halting with the right leg up to the left is also useful if the command 'Halt' is given when up against the ringside, or a door, or the chairs around the training hall. In these cases the dog will have a natural tendency to swing round for a right turn, and this movement should keep him from doing so.

Once working the dog in competition it will be realised how important this ground-work is. Quite often beginner handlers ruin their first competitive attempt because they cannot concentrate on their dogs, their footwork and the stewards commands all at once. The dog should work at a consistent pace and distance from the leg. In the showring if he is working four inches wide, the judge will probably consider this to be his normal position, however, if one minute the dog hugs the handler's leg and the next minute he is four inches away, the judge will consider the latter to be wide working. The answer is for the handler to find the position that is most comfortable and natural for the dog, and then to stick to it. Try not to keep tit-bits in the same place all the time, for when at the halt the dog will often sit crooked trying to keep his eyes on the tit-bit pocket. The same problem arises with the recall or the stay exercises when a careless hand movement might make the dog move in anticipation of his reward.

Deportment in dog training is rather like the precise schooling needed when showing a horse. The rider barely seems to twitch a muscle to convey some instruction to the horse, but the points of contact between rider and horse are more numerous than between handler and dog. The rider has the reins, his seat, thighs, calves and distribution of body weight. In the lower classes the handler has the lead and the voice. In the advanced stages of competition a lead is not used and that is when the voice and correctly maintained body deportment during training become so important. The dog must learn that the left leg gives the signals, and he must stick to it like glue. However, all the training in the world will be of no avail if the handler's deportment is poor, so remember, hold the body upright, use small steps and keep the bottom tucked in.

In all of the manoeuvres that follow, if the steps are kept small and precise and the knees as close together as possible, very little floor space will be used and there are fewer obstacles for the dog to negotiate, such as stepping back or halting on a turn. All commands should be given before the aid is applied, and in the case of a puppy, a slight delay between a command and the aids will help him to understand what is required. He will want to learn, so give him the chance to do so.

Greater detail on heelwork training will be found in a separate chapter, but once straight lines and left hand circles have been perfected and the handler is confident of full attention from the dog, turns can be practised from a stationary position. Until they have been perfected in this way, no attempt should be made to include them during heelwork. The left turn is not taught until the right and right about turns have been mastered, as the left turn can cause the dog to become apprehensive and lag. Use plenty of tit-bits and praise, and only attempt to teach one turn at a time.

THE RIGHT TURN

The command is 'Heel'. Place the left foot at a right angle across the front of the right foot with the toe pointing right. Step through to the right with the right foot, and then close up the left foot. The three aids should be used to place the dog in the sit, by transferring the lead to the right hand and pressing lightly on the dog's bottom with the left, as the command 'Sit' is given. After each exercise tuck the dog's head round your left leg so that he gets used to paying attention all the time. This is where a lot of dog handlers lose their points. They execute a very close turn, but as they do so the dog looks away and they cannot re-establish concentration without an extra command. It's not as difficult as you may think so practise the steps a few times with two paces between. You should be thinking something along these lines – one step, two steps, place the foot and turn.

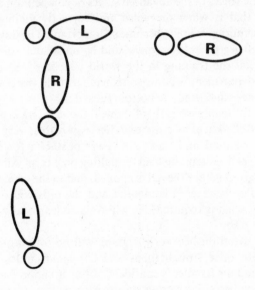

Fig. 1   The Right Turn

To give the dog all the aids needed to make a neat turn, co-ordinate the right arm with the foot movements. It should swing forward simultaneously with the movement of the left foot, swing back for the step through with the right foot, and return to the side for the halt.

THE ABOUT TURN

The command is 'Heel'. Place the left foot across the front of the right foot as for the right turn. Turn the right foot round on the spot so that it faces back the way it came, step through with the left and close up with the right. Don't forget the three aids to place the dog in the sit, and to tuck the dog's nose in to keep his attention. Practise this movement again with two paces in between until it becomes automatic.

With this manoeuvre the arms not only serve as aids to the dog but also enable balance to be maintained. The right arm should swing forward simultaneously with the movement of the left foot, swing back as the right foot is turned round, and return to the side whilst stepping through to the halt.

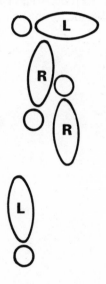

Fig. 2   The About Turn

THE LEFT TURN

The command for the left turn is 'Close'. Try not to use the word 'back' for it is a harsh sounding word and can cause the dog to be apprehensive. From the halt, place the left foot at a right angle across the toe of the right foot with the toe pointing to the left, bring the right foot round and step through. Close up to the halt with the left foot, and use the three aids to place the dog in the sit, tucking his nose round your left leg. This manoeuvre is quite tricky and difficulty may

be experienced getting the dog's body length to turn close so that you
don't fall over him. To teach him to swing his backside round and
tuck in, after placing the left foot for the turn, step back onto the
right foot before stepping through. Use the left hand as a funnel to
run the lead through, guiding the dog back before completing the
turn. This brings the dog round in a loop and allows the larger breeds,
such as Alsatians, to tuck in neatly. If, despite the step back, the dog
is still cutting the corner, instead of taking a pace backwards, take a
pace to the right with the right foot. This extra pace can be made
smaller as improvement is made.

With this movement, the right arm swings forward simultaneously
with the first step of the left foot, swings back as the right foot comes
round, and returns to the side for the halt.

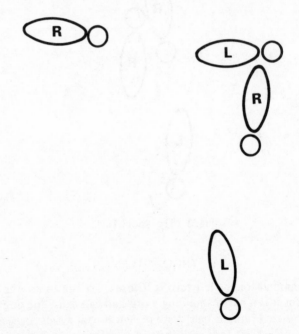

Fig. 3   The Left Turn

THE LEFT ABOUT TURN

The command is 'Close'. Place the left foot as for the left turn. Bring the right foot round and through so that it is going back the way it came, step through with the left foot and halt with the right. If difficulty is experienced with this method or if the agility of the handler is nothing but a pleasant memory, there is a second method which will be discussed next.

Arm movements for the first method are: The right arm swings left diagonally across the body with the movement of the left foot. Backwards when stepping through with the right foot, and forward for the left step, returning to the side for the halt.

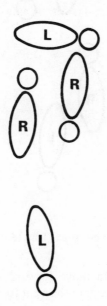

Fig. 4   The Left About Turn

THE LEFT ABOUT TURN (Second Method)

Place the left foot as for the left turn, step to the right of the left foot with the right foot. Turn the left foot so that it is facing left at a 90 degree angle to the right foot, and then step through with the right. Finally bring up the left foot for the halt.

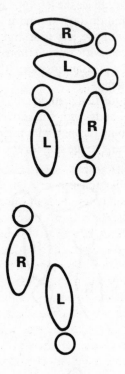

Fig. 5   The Left About Turn (Second Method)

The right arm should move forward when placing the foot, backward when stepping onto the right foot, forward when the left foot is placed and backwards for the step through with the right. It then returns to the side for the halt. Use the three aids to place the dog in the sit position, and then tuck his nose round.

The left about turn executed in this way allows the right foot to be placed wider for the handler to step back on it. Using the left hand as a funnel for the lead, the dog is turned in a loop instead of on the spot, until more familiar with the exercise.

While teaching these turns it is preferable to halt immediately they have been negotiated, but the handler must take care not to overdo it for fear of the dog expecting a halt after every turn. To stop this happening occasionally take a quick step out of the turn to continue with heelwork, which will break the sequence, avoiding the dog hanging back in anticipation of a halt. It can be taken further at the training club by the handler purposely ignoring the instructions to halt after a turn.

Dogs are likely to start working on a steward's commands once they become used to the routine or even the sounds of the commands, so a wise instructor will occasionally tell a handler to ignore all the commands he gives, with the handler making the decision of when to halt or turn. For example when a left turn is called, a right turn can be executed or the command ignored altogether. It doesn't matter what is done as long as it is different to the instructor's call. This method of training not only applies to heelwork but most exercises, and is particularly useful for all types of recall when the instruction to call the dog should sometimes be ignored. In this way, it is unlikely that a dog under test will work to the steward's commands.

Only practise the same exercise for a few moments each day, never attempting to teach him more than one manoeuvre at a time. If this rule is broken then the dog will not only lose interest, but his attention will wander. Use tit-bits and praise to let him know when he is right, ignoring mistakes when wrong. If persistently wrong, rather than reprimand, break off from work and play with him.

It is my hope that this chapter will have provided food for thought, with realisation that there is a lot more to dog training than putting the lead and chain on then having a go. Careful application of general deportment, footwork and armwork will pay great dividends in the long run. Get these things right first to give the dog a chance of learning easily, without unnecessary confusion and subsequent apprehension.

3

Heelwork

Once the handler has perfected deportment and mastered the turns without a dog, heelwork can be attempted with the dog on the lead, but first he should be taught to put his head through the training collar, ensuring that it is worn the correct way round. Once learned two purposes are served: it stops the handler becoming bad tempered and tense, chasing the puppy's head with the chain while he tries to avoid wearing it, and it gives him the idea that this is a pleasant experience.

Contrary to general practise I commence training a puppy using a training collar, for with careful sympathetic use it serves a better purpose than a leather collar. My objections to the latter are that it must be fixed very tightly to the neck to avoid the puppy wriggling out of it, also any movement of the lead will move all of the pup which is not what we require. It must be emphasised that over use of the training collar worn by a young pup will do damage. On the other hand if used cautiously from the beginning it can pay great dividends.

Lead training can be started with a sense of determination and playfulness but try not to be too serious at first. If the puppy senses that his handler is tense he may decide that this is not a game after all, he'll pop his backside down and no amount of coaxing, pushing, shouting or heaving will shift him. Such action will defeat the golden rule which is to play at it without pulling or jerking on the lead. A young pup out for his first jaunt may start pulling with over enthusiasm, but before checking him teach the correct position and meaning of the command 'Heel' by walking gently in large left circles. Whenever he moves ahead, stop and gently bring him back to the correct position with the use of the command, while running the left hand down the lead to guide him back into position. If after many attempts he still persists with pulling, or if working an older dog that has learned to incessantly pull, let him get ahead, release the lead tension, then give a hard sharp check coupled with the verbal command. It is very important that as soon as this has been done, the tension is released, allowing the training collar to slacken while immediate praise is given. With most dogs, especially pups, if this course of action becomes necessary it need only be taken once or twice. However, an older dog that has always been allowed to pull on the lead cannot be deterred by correcting once or twice, it being necessary to check him hard several times before he gives up. Many people think that this is cruel but watching two dogs, one well trained enjoying a stroll on a loose lead, and the other pulling and straining with saliva frothing from his mouth, it becomes obvious which method is cruel.

Assuming that the pup understands the meaning of the command 'Heel' and knows his position, work him in a left circle at a reasonable pace. At this stage the lead can be in either hand so that something of interest to the dog can be carried to maintain his attention. The length of each pace should be kept short and the dog should receive plenty of encouragement at all times. The encouragement can eventually be dropped to a whisper so that the dog must pay close attention. If he jumps up don't worry. Unfortunately, all too soon, some breeds, especially the larger built dogs, become bored and slow, so while the excitement is there encourage it. Work at a pace that is comfortable and don't slow down or speed up to suit the dog.

During early heelwork lessons do not incorporate sits. Remember that this is all a new experience for the dog and that he is only just learning to enjoy walking without pulling, so don't confuse, or give him any cause for worry. If during early lessons he is taught to sit at heel, apprehension is likely to set in as he doesn't know whether to walk or stop, so teach sitting at heel and paying attention as a separate exercise, using praise and tit-bits.

Once the dog works the left circle with confidence paying full attention, the circle can become more oblong so that two sides of it are straight with the bends becoming left wheels, whilst attention is maintained.

The explanations so far may give the impression that the dog should be capable of perfect heelwork after ten minutes' training, but in fact it is not like that at all. The handler should take the training slowly, only progressing to the next stage when the dog is working correctly with confidence. Walking in a line which bends first to one side and then to the other, rather as though walking in and out of a row of bollards, is the next move. Slowly the right wheels can become right turns, but progression to this 90 degree turn must be gradual otherwise the dog will lag.

Teach the right turn first, followed by the about turn, leaving the left turn until last to avoid confusing the issue. After all many hours will be spent encouraging the dog to walk close to the leg watching the handler's every move. If suddenly held back for the left turn while the handler walks across his front possibly kicking him in the process, in future he will wait to see where he should be going prior to catching up, thus apprehension of heelwork has already set in. Don't be afraid to take time, perfecting each manoeuvre before proceeding to the next. At the same time keep training sessions playful and interesting, stopping to play with him at any time he looks slightly bored, for if not very careful the result could be a reluctant worker.

A dog that lags is frustrating, aggravating, and annoying, but always the fault of the handler. There are many other ways that the dog can be taught to lag such as excessive checking with the lead which is a quick way to put a pup off heelwork for life, as is the silent massed heelwork approach of some dog training clubs. When attending a club a number of zombie dogs and people will be encountered. The people are either not really interested or they lack the confidence to encourage their bored dogs in public. Never fall into this trap, taking care to train only when feeling enthusiastic rather than because it has become a duty. Don't be afraid to talk to the dog in public, after all in a training club it should be the rule rather than the exception. If training sessions are kept short and cheerful, without any apprehension creeping in, a happy heelworker may be the result. If the dog does lag, the only real cure is a body lead. This aid can be a thick leather lead looped under his tummy with the end threaded through the handle, a wide leather collar, or anything else that can be safely used without the risk of cutting into the dog's stomach. it should be used under supervision at a training club having first allowed the dog to become accustomed to wearing it. To give the idea of how the body lead works some explanation is needed. Walk with the normal training lead held in the right hand and the body lead in the left hand, easing the dog up by the use of the body lead when he lags. The check chain must not be used to correct lagging, being confined to keeping the front half of the dog in the correct position. Neither should halts be incorporated for the fear of causing confusion about when to stop and start. Tight left turns must be avoided as they naturally encourage the dog to lag, so make sure that he has regained full confidence before reintroducing these two manoeuvres, being patient using tit-bits and a lot of praise.

With a forward working dog keep showing him the correct position by stopping and bringing him back. Another method is to loop the lead behind the legs, holding it in the right hand, for in this way the dog checks himself every time he attempts to work forward or wide. This is also very useful for the transition from heelwork on the lead, to heelfree.

Two causes of wide working are leaning over the dog and clumsy footwork. Stepping into the dog is another fault which not only creates wide heelwork but also wide sits when halting. To cure this fault, step away from the dog to the right and simultaneously check him in. Avoid stepping into the dog in the future and halt by bringing the left leg up to the right rather than vice versa, as in this way it is more difficult to step in.

Until the dog is working a straight line paying full attention don't include any halts, and when the time has come to do so don't overdo it. Use the three aids more often than not, and if the latter, be quick to ensure the dog obeys by their immediate application. A dog learns to perfect faults easily, but the use of the aids avoids the problem in the first place. If the dog is slow to sit, try tweaking a little bit of skin down his back, or flopping the lead gently over his backside. A wand can be carried behind the back to give a sharp tap on the backside, but this method must be used carefully and only for very short periods, as the dog tends to swing away to avoid the tap. Don't stop using the aids too early, for perfection of heelwork is not a race against the clock, and he will be much more reliable in the showring if never allowed to go wrong.

When taking part in massed heelwork at a training club, continual left turns in each corner will eventually teach the dog to go wide on the turn. To avoid this it is a good idea to occasionally execute an about turn and a half in the corner.

The dog that works with his hindquarters at an angle to the handler is said to be 'crabbing'. This fault can be caused by several handling mistakes such as practising too many right hand circles causing the dog's hindquarters to swing out. Carrying tit-bits in the same hand or pocket, and then giving one to the dog at each halt, will cause him to crab in an effort to watch the place where the food is hidden. Untidy or incorrect footwork on the about turn can be another reason for the problem, as the dog will swing out to avoid the handler. All these problems can be avoided if the dog understands the meaning of the command 'Close', which can be taught from quite an early age. With the dog sitting at heel, give the command 'Wait', then by stepping off with the right leg to avoid him confusing the exercise with heelwork, leave by approximately two paces. Turn to the left holding the lead in the right hand and using the left hand as a funnel, step back onto the left leg giving the command 'Close'. The dog should then be placed in the sit position, but at first it may be found necessary to take a pace forward. Whichever way it is done the three aids must be used to ensure a fast accurate sit. To advance this exercise take two paces to the right of the dog. Step back onto the left foot holding the lead in the right hand, using the left hand as a funnel for the lead to run through. Holding the lead in this manner, the left hand can run down it to near the dog's neck, guiding him in close. These exercises are, of course, very similar to those used to teach the dog the left turn with the command being the same.

When ready to try heelwork with the dog free, but not fully confident of success, or the dog works close at heel except on the turns, try the following technique. Work normally with a loose lead held in the left hand, using the arm movements practised with the footwork. Make use of the swinging right arm to catch hold of the lead close to the dog's neck, thus tightening him on each turn. This system helps to gauge the dog's accuracy without allowing him to pick up any silly habits from continually making mistakes on the right and about turns. A further advantage of this method is that the dog becomes used to seeing the right arm come across to tighten him in, so when working either heelfree or with the lead attached under competition conditions, the arm will be a constant reminder that he should keep close.

Heelfree will require a greater degree of control by voice, so holding the dog's attention by the use of encouragement becomes even more important. When working with the lead, remember that it should be held in a light and elastic manner, with the difference between tight and slack being just a flick of the wrist. An older dog that persistently jumps up can be deterred by turning left each time that he does so. This action also deters barking, however, it is the most difficult vice to cure and one that should never have been permitted to develop in the first place. Most judges will deduct marks from a barking dog, so the problem is to be avoided.

Classes 'B' and 'C' heelwork entail changes of pace. Apart from the normal walking pace, slow and fast paces are tested. Remember to keep any pace constant. For example, at a fast pace don't slow down on the turns, for once a dog changes pace from a canter to a trot, it is very difficult to get him to canter again. The same applies to the trot and the walk, and don't forget that a change of pace can mean a possible loss of attention. There are many points that the wise handler should remember such as never jerking into a different pace, particularly from the normal to the slow. The movement should be fluid, with the handler executing the change gradually over two or three steps. When training advanced heelwork, practise many changes of pace with the lead attached using different commands such as, 'Heel' for normal pace, 'Slow' for the slow pace, and 'Hurry' for the fast pace. Swing the right arm at the normal pace, hold it still to the side for the slow pace, and hold both arms to the chest for the fast pace as would a runner. Whilst at all times each pace should be constant, in training take a faster, shorter step out of any turn. This ploy will help to discourage that quick lag that dogs are prone to when coming out of a turn. However in the showring a good judge will notice such tactics and deduct marks accordingly.

When practising the fast pace with a puppy, never make a sharp left turn but rather make the turn more of a wheel. This will avoid him bumping into the leg, which will only teach him to turn wide. As the dog becomes more experienced, use the following method of footwork, which will make it easier for the dog to tuck in close. Turn the left foot slightly to the left and then take a pace to the right with the right foot. Close the left leg up to the right before stepping off again with the right foot. Ease the dog in close as you execute this movement.

Do not exaggerate this footwork in the competition ring, for a good judge will treat it as a signal to the dog, and marks will be lost.

Try not to rush any stage of heelwork. It is very easy to ruin a young dog and very difficult to rekindle a dog's enthusiasm once he is lagging. Take time when teaching each manoeuvre, and don't practise the left turn too soon as it can make the dog apprehensive. Avoid halts during heelwork until the dog is completely confident, and even at advanced stages include only a few. Dispense with one of the three aids at a time and more often than not use them all. Try not to become over confident working the dog at heel free too soon or too often. For extra accuracy and control, practise the turns from the halt and at the slow pace. Take it slowly and carefully using plenty of tit-bits and praise, and an eager, willing dog will be the result.

4

The Novice Recall and the Finish

The puppy's name and the command 'Come' should be used at mealtimes, as this immediately associates the exercise with a pleasant experience and encourages an enthusiastic reaction. How many times have you seen owners in a park or recreation area screaming and bawling at their dog to come and getting absolutely nowhere? It is an embarrassing experience for a dog owner and causes endless amusement to spectators. The answer is to teach the dog to come as a puppy and to perfect the recall before attempting it with an unsympathetic audience.

Without a recall, progress cannot be made to the more advanced training exercises, for once the dog is off the lead he is a free agent. Unless the voice binds him to the handler with respect and love, there is little hope of him returning in a retrieve, scent, or sendaway test.

It is unnecessary for the dog to have learned to sit still before the recall is first taught, in fact both the sit and the finish are better treated as separate exercises. Let's first look at the physical act of the dog returning to his handler on command. With the dog on the lead, walk with him at heel, and ensure that he is paying attention. Start walking backwards, giving the command 'Jacko Come' and flicking the lead lightly to encourage him to do so. Continue to walk backwards and, if necessary, repeat the command a couple of times to ensure the dog is aware of it. Without finishing the exercise, just break off and fuss the dog, giving him a tit-bit and praise. This exercise can be repeated frequently with plenty of praise and tit-bits to keep his interest and speed. However, each dog has his own boredom level, so as soon he looks like slowing or not treating it as a game, the time has come to stop training and to play with him instead.

To teach the dog to sit and wait, forget the recall, concentrating on making him stable. Be patient at this stage because a young dog can lack confidence, so that when the handler tries to walk away his first instinct is to follow. With the dog on the lead place him in the sit, at the heel position. Hold the lead in the right hand and let it run over the left hand, keeping the collar slightly taut. Using the right leg, step slightly away from the dog before moving round in front to face him, no more than a pace away from his nose. Use the command 'Wait'. After very few attempts, relax the pressure on the collar, but be ready to flick the left hand back up under the lead, so that it runs straight up above his head if he shows any sign of moving. Return to the dog's side, initially after a very short period, for it takes a little while for the dog to learn to sit still when the handler is not beside him. However, he will slowly become more stable and then the exercise can be taken one stage further. Take two or three paces away from the dog's nose, and then after a very short interval return and stand straight, right in front of his nose, so that he is in a perfect present position. Walk round the dog in a left hand direction to the heel position, ensuring that the lead is kept taut above his head. Thus the dog has been taught several things. Sitting still on command, the correct present position, the correct finish position, and at no time has he been required to move!

When all of these exercises have been perfected the handler can attempt to put them together. With the dog on the lead, place him at heel in the sit position and tell him to 'Wait'. Leave the dog by a lead's length, stepping to the right whilst doing so, then face him, remaining stationary before flicking both hands towards the groin giving the command 'Jacko Come'. At first it may be found that the dog is more stable if backed away from, thus the handler is in a position to quickly say 'Wait' again. When the hands are flicked to the groin, this will have the effect of flicking the lead and bringing the dog into a stand. It is important to give the command simultaneously with the hand movement, otherwise he will become apprehensive and will hesitate before coming. Once the dog has arrived in front, walk back if necessary to straighten him up before giving the command 'Sit', and then walk round to the heel position. If the dog is slow to sit at the present, quickly lean forward and tap his backside, but only do this once or twice or he will sit well away. Don't pull the dog in on the lead. If he hesitates a flick of the lead will be sufficient. If he is really apprehensive, a visible 'tit-bit' could also be useful, but the handler must take the blame for the apprehension will have been caused by poor training, such as a heavy jerk of the lead, bad timing, too harsh a tone of voice, or using the aids in the wrong order. Remember to use the dog's name followed by the command 'Come', then immediately slightly tighten the lead. Speed will follow the use of correctly applied aids.

Straightening the dog before giving the command to sit is difficult. The handler should try to avoid twisting the body or grabbing the dog's head, as the latter action will only encourage him to sit back in apprehension of the hands. So stand upright with the feet about nine inches apart, give the command, flick the hands into the groin, and as the dog approaches lean slightly back and draw them up to the chest. The dog will probably watch the hands, especially if a tit-bit has been secreted there every now and again. Avoid waving them around, or leaving them too low, as it will be difficult to attract the dog's attention if he is looking straight down instead of at the handler's face. Remember that a dog can be sitting perfectly straight, but will look to be crooked because his head is not upright. If the dog wanders to one side, walk backwards in the opposite direction encouraging him to come in straight.

The finish is the final part of the exercise, which the dog can fail even when the basics have been mastered. It is always better to teach it as a separate exercise, and this can be practised in confined areas. Stand with the dog sitting in the present position, holding the lead in the left hand looped behind the right knee. Give the command 'Heel' and take a step back with the right leg thus tightening the lead. This will have the effect of bringing him forward. Encourage him round, take a step forward with the right leg, changing the lead to the right hand so as to be able to use the three aids for the sit, then tuck his head round the left leg to maintain attention. Don't be worried if at first the dog does not get up and walk round. Take several steps forward, calling his name and the command 'Heel', while tapping the left leg to indicate the correct position. Once shown this exercise the dog will soon learn and it will start to become easier. Don't forget the praise! When the dog becomes reasonably proficient it can be developed further. With the dog sitting in the present positon, the lead should be looped down in front of the handler and held in the left hand. Give the command 'Heel' and as he goes round, the lead will follow him round the legs and tighten, therefore encouraging him to sit close in the heel position. It may be found necessary to first take a step back onto the right leg, but eventually it will be possible to leave this part of the move out. Don't forget the three aids to place him in the sit.

An alternative is to teach the dog the left hand finish. To do so start with the dog in the present position. The lead should be slack and held in the right hand. Give the command 'Close' and simultaneously take a step back with the left leg, running the left hand down the lead to his neck. This will take the dog in a left circle, and as the left leg is returned the dog is brought to heel. As he does so apply the three aids for a smart straight sit.

Avoid standing with the feet at ten to two, as this will encourage the dog to sit crooked, both in the present position and at heel. The finish must not be used with the recall every time, or it will be found that the dog will sit crooked or off centre in anticipation of the command. Quite often finish by walking round the dog to the heel position thus leaving him stationary, say, 'Good Dog' then let him relax. This way the dog won't always be expecting the same thing, and one cause of crooked sits can be avoided. Once the dog has mastered the whole recall exercise, occasionally go back to short recalls on the lead, otherwise the dog may slow up having lost interest.

An ideal way of practising the recall and getting straight sits every time is to work the dog in what are known as 'tapes', but never do so with a dog of under twelve months of age. To erect tapes at home only stakes and some string are necessary, however, if metal is used for the stakes, bend the tops over, making them safe for both dog and handler. Set up two rows so that they make an avenue sufficiently wide for just dog and handler, then tie string along each side at about mid calf to knee level. The first step is to teach the dog to respect the tapes so that he doesn't jump over or crawl under them. Put him on the lead and walk into the avenue with the dog at heel. As soon as he sniffs the tapes or attempts to escape from them, check him and say 'No'. To ensure that he understands, it may be necessary to do this once or twice before the recall is practised. When first leaving him, it is inadvisable to go too far, but rather try several recalls standing a short distance from the dog. Should greater accuracy be required, stand with the legs outside the tapes thus straddling them, so that the legs can be slowly drawn together decreasing the width of the channel during the recall. This will have the effect of funnelling the dog straight into the perfect present position without allowing him to sit crooked. With the tapes so close to him it will be impossible to practise a finish, so do not attempt to do so.

In later stages it will be found necessary for the dog to be able to sit straight in front of the handler when called from any angle, therefore angled recalls become essential training. With the lead attached, place the dog in the heel position, then walk to the end of the lead, but instead of remaining directly in front of him, take two paces to the left or the right. If starting from the right, give the command 'Come', flicking the lead across to the right which will ensure that the dog moves in the correct direction. As this is done, step back with the right leg, leaving the left leg straight out in front, then draw the hands up whilst leaning slightly back. The leg, acting as a barrier, will encourage the dog to come round it to sit in front, with the hands and posture of the body encouraging a close present. The same method is used for the left angled recall leaving the right leg to guide the dog in. It is important that the leg used as a barrier is returned rather than taking a pace forward with the other foot.

If the dog is slow to come at training classes, stop practising lead-free recalls for a little while, concentrating on short lead attached ones, without a finish at the end. With the use of lavish praise and tit-bits, interest will soon be rekindled so that he will be able to go back to classwork before long. Never let anyone go behind a reluctant dog to clap or give a helping tow, as this will only make him nervous when sitting, resulting in broken stays as well as not coming when called.

The handler may be in the happy position of owning a dog that anticipates the recall. It is not a cause for worry as this kind of enthusiasm is uncommon and is classed as a good fault. For sufficient control of anticipation in the showring, at training classes a step can be taken towards the dog as those on either side of him are called by their respective handlers. By doing so it becomes unnecessary to repeat the command, just the movement of the handler should keep him steady, but if he does move call him in, and never return to push him back into place. During training, the dog that persistently anticipates after the handler has faced him, and particularly after the instructor says 'call your dog', only needs to learn the meaning of the command 'Wait'. Rather than call him, the handler should return to stand at the present position before he has moved. With the dog that doesn't let the handler get away at all, or not very far before moving, practise many sits on the lead, only gradually moving away as he gains confidence. If it is possible to get away before he moves, try leaving, and then return to walk once round him, repeating the command 'Wait' as the dog is left for the sequence to be repeated. Gradually the distance between dog and handler can be lengthened, but it takes much patience, practising for short periods without ever ending the sessions on an angry note. This is easily said, but as far as possible it must be so, even when the dog has been persistently wrong. It is far better to forget the exercise that is wrong, practising one short exercise that he can perfect, so that praise can be given, then the training session ended with play. In such a way the next time he is approached for training his memories of the previous session will be pleasant.

5

The Retrieve

Everyone dreams of having a natural retriever, but in fact the only reliable retrieve will be one that has been taught. To do so it is necessary to partially discourage the natural instinct for retrieving, then to teach the dog from the beginning. This sounds a little brutal but it doesn't have to be. Dogs can be forced to retrieve without cruelty, being firm and systematic instead.

Long before serious retrieve training commences it is a good idea to start the puppy holding easy articles just as soon as he cuts his adult teeth. If using a dumb-bell, wrap something soft round the mouthpiece, or for preference use an article more pliable, such as felt glove with the fingers rolled up. Care must be taken not to ram the article into the back of the dog's jaws or to damage his mouth in any way, as this will not only discourage a natural retrieve, but put him off for life!

To teach the simple command 'Hold It' the handler should be positioned on a chair, with the dog sitting between the knees, and the lead secured so that his freedom is restricted. It may be found a little easier, with less strain on the back, if a small dog is placed on a table. Once in the chosen position, offer the dumb-bell to the dog giving the command 'Hold It'. He will almost certainly turn his head away or just look at it, so now is the time to persuade the dog to open his mouth. This can be done by placing the left hand under or over the dog's jaw pushing the loose skin of his mouth towards his teeth, thus having the effect of making him open his jaws. With the right hand, place the retrieve article in his mouth giving the command 'Hold It', then use the same hand to hold the loose flesh under his throat slightly lifting his head. In this way it becomes impossible for the article to be ejected. The left hand is now free to caress the dog over the head whilst he is told how clever he is. However, if he struggles the command should be repeated in a firm manner, followed immediately by praise. This can mean that the handler has to switch from praise to being firm in a split second. Some dogs will be stubborn, endeavouring to wriggle away, but this is why the lead must restrict the movements. Keep repeating the command interspersed with praise before using the word 'Give', followed by a tit-bit, so that the experience is not remembered as being distasteful.

It may be found that the dog locks his jaw on the article in such a way that it cannot be prised from him, this is quite understandable for he has yet to learn that the article must be released at the handler's request. It is just as important for the dog to learn this right at the beginning as it is for him to learn to hold. At dog shows, occasionally a handler can be seen to be having difficulty removing an article or scent cloth from their dog's mouth. Whilst excuses are given for their dog's behaviour, the fact remains that the problem should never have been allowed to develop in the first place. So at the first sign of the jaw being locked, just put the forefinger in the side of the dog's mouth, behind the article where there is a gap in the teeth, and take it whilst repeating the command 'Give'. The whole performance will have to be repeated many times, so that eventually when the retrieve article is placed in front of the dog's face and the command 'Hold It' given, he will open his mouth of his own free will whilst leaning forward to take it.

Assuming that for several weeks this method has been used every day without the dog opening his mouth voluntarily, other methods will have to be considered. So far the handler has opened the dog's mouth which he might be prepared to accept forever. This being so it will mean that an alternative method of opening the jaws without the fingers being used is required. One such method is to use the forefinger and thumb of the left hand to close his nostrils, which will have the effect of shutting off his air supply. To continue to breathe he must open his mouth, when the article can be placed inside with the loose skin under the throat being held as explained previously. Immediate genuine and profuse praise must be given so that he is left in no doubt that he is acting correctly. After a while, if the forefinger and thumb are placed near the dog's nose whilst the command is given simultaneously, he will open his mouth voluntarily, when the same amount of praise should be used. If he takes time to learn, just persevere without worrying as some dogs get the idea after just a few attempts, whilst others will try the patience over a long period of time.

Some people think that if they own a natural retriever they can afford to leave this exercise to chance, congratulating themselves on their good fortune. Such good fortune deserts them when the day comes for the dog not be in the mood to retrieve, and why should he when never taught to do so. In such cases there is nothing the handler can do except go home and do what should have been done before even considering an entry at a dog show, teaching the dog to retrieve on command rather than doing it for his own pleasure. So for competition a taught retrieve is a must, it being like pressing the button on a computer for a known response. Once the dog has been taught to hold the article, using praise and tit-bits to coax him along, the time comes for the pick up from the ground to be learned. This can be accomplished in easy stages, starting by walking the dog at heel in left circles whilst he carries the article. Serving two purposes, it teaches the dog to carry the article whilst walking, and also to hold it until told to do otherwise. Once proficient at this simple task, the dog should be walked in left circles with the command 'Hold It' being given whilst the handler offers the article to him at his head level. The progression of this procedure is to lower it gradually until eventually it is almost at ground level. Once the dog has reached this stage with confidence, the tactics are slightly changed with the left circle being continued but the article being placed on the ground, so that dog and handler reach it en-route. When approaching it the command 'Hold It' is given, whereupon the dog should reach down and pick it up, but failing to do so the nostrils are closed and the article scooped into the mouth. It cannot be over stressed that the dog must be the one to pick it up and not the handler, for once starting this game the dog will always expect it and all the good work so far has been wasted. Do not think that kicking the article will help any time it is dropped, just make it a little unpleasant, insisting that the dog does the work and not the handler, then he will respect the command.

Ideally, the first thing that the dog sees when he picks up the dumb-bell is the handler standing with the hands held in the recall position, so to ensure that this happens, train the dog to go round the far side of the dumb-bell to pick up, rather than do so whilst still going away. To teach this manoeuvre, leave the dog as if for a recall on lead, then place the dumb-bell in the middle and call him, giving the command

'Hold It' at the appropriate time of approach. As soon as the dumb-bell is picked up, hook the lead under it so that it cannot be dropped. Another method of achieving the far side pick up is for the dumb-bell to be placed on the ground approximately two paces in front of the handler, and as the dog goes towards it on command, a step forward is taken in such a manner as to leave the left foot almost touching the far side of the dumb-bell. This move ensures that the dog will pick up from the far side, and is one of the Hearthrug Tips mentioned towards the end of this book, taking little room or time to practise. Another profit from the far sided pick up is that if the dumb-bell or article has been accurately thrown in a straight line from the handler, the dog has made his turn towards the handler prior to the pick up, and is therefore not returning at an angle.

Over the years I have noticed that dogs taught to pick up from the far side of the article rarely mouth or anticipate the exercise, whereas both of these faults are often encountered when the dog has not been taught to do so.

Because class instructors continually remind their dog handlers to praise the dog, it is natural that this is done as soon as the dog has the dumb-bell in his mouth. Nothing could be worse than this practise, for invariably it will distract the dog from the task in hand to the possibility of a tit-bit, thus he spits it out, rushing up to the handler for the reward. Rather than make this mistake, call his name urgently ensuring that the hands are in the recall position, but be sure that his name is not called before the pick up is complete or he will return without bringing anything. The use of just his name called in an urgent manner will facilitate a speedy return, which if used in training consistently, by the time the dog reaches the higher classes a smart return will be automatic without the extra command.

Do not use his name when sending the dog out. The command 'Hold It' is sufficient, anything else being likely to distract him from the required task with confusion also being possible. Another reason for the command only is the possible lapse of memory when the dog looks at the handler instead of continuing to mark the place where the article has fallen, but we will shortly look at the advantage of teaching the dog to mark. Before doing so, a summary of the commands and the order in which they should be given might be helpful. First tell the dog to 'Wait', and having thrown the article give the command 'Hold It', then when the dog is on the way out, put the hands in the recall position. Call his name urgently immediately the dumb-bell or article has been picked up, and when the dog has sat in the present position tell him to 'Give' so that the article is released. At this juncture perhaps I should point out that if the word leave is used by the handler for stopping the dog doing something undesirable, it is unwise for its use to also mean 'give up the article'. The former usage is often associated with rebuke, and therefore using it in conjunction with the retrieve risks apprehension.

The present to the handler by the dog with the dumb-bell in his mouth should be practised by the use of short recalls on the lead with the finish excluded. This is another Hearthrug Tip that can be used for the dog that is slow to return to the handler, and being on the lead ensures a more accurate present, providing that the aids are used. Also if the lead is hooked under the dumb-bell there is less risk of the dog ejecting it from his mouth.

With the dumb-bell retained in the dog's mouth, the finish can be used as a means of continuing the part of the exercise where the dumb-bell is held, thus reducing the risk of anticipation of the take which can precipitate dropping. The finish after the article has been taken should only be used occasionally, for as with the recall exercise, there is a risk of the dog sitting crooked in anticipation of the direction he will be required to go.

When progressing from the soft article to a dumb-bell, ensure that the mouthpiece has plenty of clearance from the ground. Height can be added to a standard dumb-bell by attaching larger squares of plywood to the ends, which will only add a little extra weight whilst giving greater clearance between the ground and the mouthpiece. It is not advisable to commence training with an article that is too big and clumsy for a small dog, and experiments with size and weight should only be made once the dog is confidently retrieving. Only throw the dumb-bell with the right hand, thus avoiding the possibility of hurting the dog's ear and the subsequent inattention that will be caused. It is a fallacy that the dog's attention is maintained by a left hand throw.

Teaching the dog to mark the fall of the article should be treated as a separate exercise. In some ways it is better taught whilst the dog is still a puppy as it can be a great game. Certainly it is not necessary for the dog to be retrieving first. To commence teaching this important part of the exercise, tie the dumb-bell, or a toy, or anything in which the dog shows interest, onto a long piece of thin string. Black thread is ideal, but not essential. Holding the end of the string in the right hand, place the dog in the heel position, then to start with throw the article just a few feet away. The very act of the throw should arouse his interest when the command 'Mark It' is given in conjunction with jerky pulls on the string. This will make the article move, and each time that it does, his interest will be rekindled. As the dog gets the idea the throw can be lengthened gradually until the string can be dispensed with altogether. When in the showring, give the command 'Mark It' whilst waiting to send the dog, and if the training has been careful he will know exactly where the article is. Of course, in the advanced classes extra commands cannot be given, but by this stage the dog should mark automatically. Don't neglect to teach this part of the exercise as dogs that have been taught to mark have an advantage over those that haven't, particularly when small articles are used where the grass is long.

Once the dog has become a confident retriever, all sorts of dumb-bells can be used. One can have a mouthpiece that can be altered, making one side lower than the other. This is a useful method of curing the dog that mouths articles, for he will have to pick up the dumb-bell correctly or he will drop it. In classes 'B' and 'C' the dog is required to retrieve an article supplied by the judge, and whilst they can be made of any material, metal articles are quite often used. Many dogs will retrieve metal without a second thought, and some object, refusing to pick up. Whatever the dog's reaction, it is wise to introduce it to him gradually. One method is to wrap tinfoil round the mouthpiece of his own dumb-bell, which while incorporating metal will be familiar to him. Another is to acquire a metal dumb-bell, first throwing his wooden dumb-bell once or twice before throwing the metal one. With luck, the dog will not stop to think about this strange article, returning with it quite happily.

In the more advanced classes, when being offered the article by the steward, always take it from the position of the article from which it is preferable for the dog to pick up, which will usually be the centre. The reason for this is that dogs are more likely to pick up from the part of the article containing a familiar scent, which gives the handler the opportunity of predetermining the point of balance. If the judge has supplied two articles tied together handle both of them, for some dogs will first pick up the unscented half, only to drop the article having detected the handler's scent on the other half.

One way to prepare the dog for the many different articles he will be asked to retrieve during his competitive career, is to discretely collect some whilst at shows. Many handlers make quite a sport of teaching their dogs to pick up really unusual things, and the variety that can be acquired in this way is quite amazing. To effect the transition from the dog's familiar dumb-bell to strange articles, wrap a piece of rag round his dumb-bell then the same rag can be wrapped round, or tucked into strange articles. The dog will have more confidence, for although he may never have previously encountered the strange article, he will detect his own scent and that of the handler upon it.

Many handlers find that their downfall is after they have thrown the article and are waiting to send the dog. Some judges require a long pause between the commands 'Wait' and 'Hold It', and in a crowded hall where many people are working dogs, and stewards are shouting instructions, it can be very distracting. The dog can forget where the article was thrown or what he has been sent to fetch, so that when he is a confident retriever in the quiet of his home, he should then be accustomed to distractions at the dog training club.

It is also advisable to ask the club instructor to call the command to send the dog, but when he has done so wait a few seconds before carrying out the instruction, thus avoiding the possibility of the dog becoming accustomed to working on the steward's command.

As with the recall, the retrieve is a basis for future exercises, so it must be reliable. If the dog anticipates the retrieve don't reprimand him, but in future, tell him to 'Wait' then retrieve the article yourself. It is a good fault that some eager dogs have, and many handlers would give anything for a dog that is keen. Anticipation is more often than not caused by habit, the dog not even hearing the command. This habit can be broken by doing something unexpected, then it will be found that the dog will listen to the command more attentively.

Tapes can be used to achieve a straight present and a close finish, but if they are not available various household objects are suitable, such as kitchen chairs placed on their sides. Angled retrieves can also be taught in this way.

Mouthing he article can become a real problem, with the dog continually losing marks for this fault in both the retrieve and scent tests. Many years ago I asked an experienced trainer how I could stop my dog mouthing. Naturally I expected gems of wisdom to pour from his lips, but his answer was, 'I don't know. My dogs are never allowed to start it in the first place'! This is really sound advice, but if training a mouthing dog, or one that picks up the dumb-bell by the end, use an unevenly weighted, or alternatively a heavy one.

If the training methods described in this chapter are used slowly and wisely, it will be possible to have a reliable retrieve, with a good basis to start training the dog for Class A scent discrimination.

they won't play they won't work.

teaching the dog wide about turns,
ote totally incorrect deportment.

The use of the body lead for lagging

Curing forward working;
lead behind keees

Greyvalley Kathy –
her first attention lesson.

The right and right about turn.
Note foot, lead and hand aids.

Heelaway Yoakil learning to sit still.
Handler walking round dog.

Recall lessons.

Recall lessons. Note straight sit.

Straight present from an angled recall using tapes.

Sealight Basil Brush learning the conventional finish – note use of lead.

Commencing the left hand finish.

The progression of the left hand finish.

Temperament test training –
dog and handler.

Temperament test training –
with a stranger.

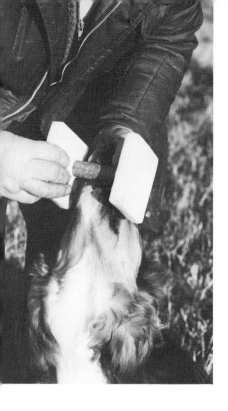

Opening the dog's mouth for the dumb-bell.

Learning to release the dumb-bell. Note use of forefingers.

The far side pick up using the foot.

The far side pick up.
Dumb-bell between dog and handler.

Teaching Class A Scent discrimination.
Note paper tents and irretrievable articles.

Class B Scent discrimination.
Rags pegged onto a line so
dog cannot make a mistake.

Obscuring all vision.

Look straight for the sendaway.

Handler in position – vision still obscured.

he hands finally acting as blinkers.

. Ch. Sealight Rogue
owing how he was taught the sendaway.
te seven alternatives in one.

Distant Control Training

(a) Sit to the Down.

(b) Down to the Sit.

Distant Control Training

(c) Sit to the Stand.

(d) Stand to the Sit.

Distant Control Training

(e) Stand to the Down.

(f) Down to the Stand, first movement.

(Fig. c shows second movement)

6

The Stays and the Temperament Test

It is a wonder that a dog learns anything at all considering all the contradictions involved. One moment he is left in the sit, then he is recalled, then for a stay exercise he is left only to be reprimanded for returning to the handler. It doesn't finish there for the dog thinks that he is required to remain sitting, and then his handler tells him that he must lie down. Really, it is quite probable that a human would go mad under such conflicting instructions. Be that as it may, we want the dog to do all of these things, and so it is extremely important that we try to make each exercise as easy and clear as possible. The first rule with stay exercises is never practise them immediately before or after recalling the dog. This simple rule applies to all dogs no matter how advanced. Always be helpful to the dog and avoid confusion, as you are the one who loses if you make it difficult for him.

To start teaching this exercise place the dog in the sit position and stand beside him. Give him the command 'Sit Stay', then leave him by taking a pace slightly to the right with your right foot prior to facing him. Hold the lead in the right hand and use the left hand as a funnel, the lead should run straight up from the dog's neck thus holding him in the sit. At first stand so that you are just in front of the dog's nose and, repeating the command 'Sit Stay', slowly loosen the training collar by lowering the left hand. If there is any shuffling or paw moving, then the left hand must immediately lift the lead up again leaving no room for movement, and the command must be repeated firmly. As soon as the dog is settled it should be followed by 'Good Boy' and, again, a slackening of the collar. Only leave him for a few seconds at a time to begin with, for if you wait until the dog stands or shuffles, he is only being encouraged to be unsteady or to break his stays. Start off by standing right up to the dog's nose, trying to make him maintain the sit position for, let's say fifteen seconds. If fifteen seconds doesn't sound long, just try keeping a young pup in the sit for that length of time when he has never tried a stay exercise before! Time never moves so slowly as it does when leaving an unsteady dog, and the heart misses every other beat wondering if a prize is being thrown away because the dog has not been carefully taught. Don't put yourself in this position, start while the pup is young and never let him go wrong. Only when a pup is steady in a short stay with the handler in front of him can the duration be lengthened, and only when perfectly steady on a loose lead should an attempt be made to move away. To do so, leave the dog and face him close to his nose, then take one step back, but use the hands in the same way to keep him steady. Don't rush it. Taking paces away from the dog before he is confident is disastrous and will surely ruin him, perfection for short periods being the aim.

Many handlers get their hands in an awful knot during stay exercises. The trouble they have keeping them out of the way would lead one to believe that they had as many arms as an octopus. Don't clasp the hands in front, as this is the recall sign, guaranteed to signal a well trained dog out of his position. Neither should the hands be clasped behind the back, for when the judge says 'backs to your dogs' the hands are back in the recall position! Try to either keep them by the sides, or folded and avoid putting them in pockets, as dogs have marvellous memories of the whereabouts of tit-bits. Having established that the hands and arms can teach the dog bad habits, progress the sit-stay to its next stage. There has to be a point when he is taken off the lead and left at a distance, and with all the careful basic training that has been given, this should not present any problems. Of course in a hall full of distractions it is quite possible that the most reliable dog will break his stays. In these circumstances don't correct the dog yourself, get a friend in the training club to put him back in the correct position, repeating the command. This should not be done by strangers to the dog, particularly stay stewards at a dog show, unless the handler specifically asks them to do so. The same rule applies to the dog that barks, by returning to correct him a 'handler's recall' has been performed, and by this I mean the case of the dog that learns to bark whilst left in a stay, knowing that the handler will return, and this is just what he wants.

Most dogs will fight the act of being placed in the down until they understand it. It is best not to fuss or overhandle them, as this only makes matters worse. When first attempting to put the dog into the down, stand across him at a slight angle whilst he is in the sit position, then loop the lead so that it nearly touches the floor. Position the left foot as high up the lead and as near the dog's neck as possible, then put the foot to the ground taking the pressure of the lead with the right hand until he goes down. As this is done give the command 'Down'. Do not remove the foot at first but go down and stroke the dog's head telling him how clever he is. Even if the dog wriggles do not move but keep the foot there and repeat the comand, he will soon find it more comfortable to keep still. Slowly it will be found that the lead pressure can be released and the lead can be laid out on the ground, enabling the handler to move away from the dog whilst still maintaining a certain amount of control over his movements. This stage must not be rushed as once the dog breaks the exercise it is difficult to correct, so do not allow mistakes to happen. Should the dog become unsteady, revert to standing on the lead near his neck so that he cannot move. In all stay exercises it is advisable to maintain the dog's attention, but whatever you do to achieve this don't say the dog's name, but rather click the fingers or make an interesting noise. This is an added 'safety valve', as some dogs start sniffing and in the sit-stay go down, attempting to get nearer to what interests them. In the down-stay this same problem causes them to creep forward on their tummies to the next interesting smell. Sometimes the sniffing leads them to another dog, and then someone else's stay has also been ruined, so try to keep the dog's attention so that smells and other dogs are not so interesting.

The first stays out of sight of the dog will probably be attempted at home, and at first it should only be a case of walking out of sight and then immediately returning. The period of absence can be gradually lengthened until the dog is stable for long periods. However, keep popping back or looking through cracks in the doors so that the dog is looking for his handler's return. This may seem strange when what is wanted is a steady dog and this approach sometimes encourages mistakes, but remember that whilst the dog is looking for his handler he is less likely to be distracted, therefore remembering what he should be doing. It also means that if used to seeing his handler walk in and out during the stays, he is less likely to move as he is returned to.

If the dog persistently breaks either exercise, go back to the basics using the lead. Sometimes dogs can form the habit of only moving in the stays under competition conditions, in which case it is necessary to throw away some marks and pop him on the lead so that it cannot happen. Most judges are very co-operative about training in the ring as long as it is realised that the marks will be forfeited. Remember that it is no good reprimanding the dog for breaking a stay exercise, just practise on the lead until it is perfect.

It is necessary to teach the dog to stand before entering the Novice class where temperament is tested with the dog in this position. Admittedly, at this stage it is not strictly a stand-stay test, but only an integral part of the Temperament Test, which we will come to later in the chapter. Class B does have a stand-stay test, and so for both of these classes we have to find a way of teaching the dog to take this position on command. To do so, the handler should stand so that the dog is sitting at right angles to him. With the lead in the left hand, hold it above but slightly back from his head, so that he is encouraged to stand by moving his back legs rather than taking a step forward. As an added aid to coax the dog up, use the left toe of the left foot under his tummy. The hand can be used to do this, but the advantage of using the foot is that the handler remains upright and the dog cannot sit with the foot in position. Some dogs will act foot shy and move away from this action, but this can be overcome by standing the dog by a wall or a chair. As progress is made, the lead can be taken off whilst the foot aid is retained, and gradually all aids can be dispensed with as the dog will immediately respond to the command 'Stand'.

Dogs that break the stay exercises are heart-breaking to the handler. In the junior classes these tests are usually the last, and if the dog moves having previously been in the lead, there is a temptation to lose the temper. This must not happen, for remember that the dog is subject to great distraction with a ring full of strange dogs, some shuffling, perhaps crying, or worse still, wandering about. So have patience, and go back to the basics on the lead so that he cannot go wrong.

Trying to rush the training of this exercise will only result in disappointment. Short periods of perfection should be aimed for. If owning a nervous or excitable dog, such short periods can be very rewarding and before long can be linked to form quite a long exercise. With a nervous dog, or one that spends all day at home with his handler, take into consideration the fact that he is not used to being left, or that he lacks the confidence to be left. If he cannot be left at home in a separate room without doors being scratched or whining, try tying him down low so that he cannot break the exercise, then go into the other room, perhaps leaving the door open. At first this should be done for very short periods so as not to cause distress, but try building it up so that his confidence grows and he is used to being alone. With all stay exercises get the dog used to staying still by walking once round him after the exercise is finished, then fuss him quietly in that position moving him off the spot *back* towards you. The reason for the emphasis on moving the dog *back* as opposed to forward is that when training for Distant Control, the dog will not have been taught the bad habit of walking forward to stand. Always make plenty of fuss of the steady dog, but never fall into the trap of giving tit-bits on return for he will soon learn to hop up in anticipation.

Take stay training slowly, teaching in a painstaking manner and full marks will be the reward in competition.

THE TEMPERAMENT TEST

Dogs should be trained for the Temperament Test and the best place for such training is at a dog training club. Once the dog has been taught to stand the handler should give him the command to adopt this position, and when steady go to the length of the lead facing him. The handler should then approach the dog from the front gently stroking him from head to tail. Once the dog accepts this he can be approached from both sides, the handler returning to the heel position each time. The next stage is for him to be placed in a line of other dogs spaced approximately one yard apart, with the handlers standing at the heel position. On command from the class instructor all handlers should go to the end of the lead facing their dogs, and approaching them from the front stroke them before returning to the heel position. The next move is for all handlers to go to the length of the lead and face their dogs. On command of the class instructor, the handlers should take two paces to the left. They will then be in front of the dog next to their own who will be approached and stroked by another handler less familiar to their own dog. The same procedure can now be carried out by the handlers taking two paces to the right, thus someone else will handle their dog.

When the instructor is satisfied that the dog accepts being handled by other people without any sign of fear or aggression, he can test the dog himself, acting as the judge would in the showring. In this way the dog is taught to accept the Temperament Test as something quite natural, and if the training has been thorough the test should hold no fear for him.

7

Class A

Moving from Novice to Class A is probably the greatest change experienced with handling technique. Many handlers ruin their dogs in the process because they will not take their time teaching the dog to work with fewer and fewer aids, and also because they will not risk the possibility of losing a place for the sake of perfecting their dog. This approach returns bad results in the future, because all the exercises taught to the dog so that he can be entered in the classes below 'A' is the basic training for the advanced work. With everyday training try leaving out one aid at a time, but not all of them. Don't be afraid to correct the dog, even in the ring, and this does not only apply to the first few entries in class A, it means at all times. Once the dog thinks that he can get away with mistakes in the ring, he will attempt it regularly. So right from the start establish who's boss and do not accept any nonsense from him in or out of the ring. Go into the first few Class A competitions with a view to using it as a training session, leaving one aid out at each stage. You should already be doing less talking to the dog, but on the occasions when doing so remember what a strong and useful aid the voice is. At this stage in training continue to use at least one aid.

Don't train the dog on too loose a lead, it can be tempting to rush training when the dog is still only capable of working with confidence in the Novice Class. If the dog is working in the Novice Class with the verbal and physical aids used during his early training, don't attempt a higher class. By the time the dog is ready for Class A he should be working the Novice Class with little verbal encouragement and with as few body aids as possible. Such aids are difficult habits to lose, as will be found, especially if the dog has been in the Beginner and

Novice Classes for some time. They become so automatic that most of the time the handler is not aware of using them. For example, dropping the left shoulder when making a left turn, a hang-over from when the left arm went back to guide the dog in close, waving body movements to get a straight present from the dog at the end of the recall, or as the dog returns from the retrieve etc. These are all traps which are there for the beginner handler to fall into. After the dog has won his first Novice Class start working with less verbal contact, don't expect to go into Class A and drop all aids at once, they must continue with a gradual decline.

Once the dog has won two Beginner Classes and is steady in the stay exercises, he can be taught the Class A recall. Remember that the way to avoid slow recalls is to practise them continually, using the following method which is part of 'Hearthrug Training'. Place the dog on the lead sitting at heel. Tell him to 'Wait' and leave him, stepping off with the right leg. When reaching the end of the lead call 'Jacko Heel' and flick it in the same way as was used for the Novice recall, but keep walking at normal heelwork pace. Do this until the dog knows what is required and is beating the flick. Then proceed with the dog still on the lead, turning left after a few paces and calling him so that he learns to come up to the left hand side. After a while unclip the lead and leave the dog for greater distances before calling him and turning left. If there is any sign of hesitation put the dog on the lead and practise short recalls with tit-bits and praise to make it more fun. However, if training is progressing smoothly at this stage, try an immediate right turn the moment the dog catches up.

To proceed with the training of this exercise, put the dog back on the lead and leave him with the command 'Wait', and when reaching the end of the lead face to the right. Call the dog, and if necessary give a quick flick of the lead, then sit him neatly in the heel position. Don't be afraid to take a pace forward to bring him right round.

To start practising lead-free, leave the dog a short distance away then call him and keep walking straight, and when he has progressed call him after making a right turn. Don't make the dog sit every time he catches up, but step backwards and break the exercise or go into a little heelwork. Don't leave the dog for the Class A recall and meander round the hall before calling him, as this is guaranteed to slow him up. He is likely to wait until the instructor or steward says 'Halt', then get up casually trotting over to sit, invariably perfectly straight at heel. So the answer is short fast recalls with no definite end. On the occasions when finishing the exercise with a sit, try halting in front of doors, gaps in rows of chairs, or in front of spectators. This will help to dispel the apprehension which many dogs have when halting near the judge, the spectators or the ring entrance. Also get someone to shout 'Halt' once the dog is walking at heel again, but keep walking so that he learns to ignore the steward's commands.

When given the command to call the dog, always wait one or two seconds before doing so, as anticipation is one of the most common faults with the Class A recall. If anticipation has become a problem, then rather than call him to heel return to him, then practise something else, as keeping the dog still is the problem not the recall. Also if in front of an obstacle, adjust the pace so that the halt is made by bringing the right leg up to the left, this should avoid the dog going past his handler in anticipation of a right turn. Finally, when turning left with a dog that is so quick that he crashes into the handler's legs, take smaller paces so that he catches up before the turn.

Remember that as Class A is the first of the more advanced classes, it is important to attain a high standard of basic training and therefore worth the time and effort to ensure that the dog enjoys and understands the exercise. The next major test to be conquered in Class A is Scent Discrimination, which will be dealt with in the next chapter.

8

Scent Discrimination

This is an exercise that can be started with a young pup. It can be taught with great fun and will remain so if time and care are taken. When the pup will chase after a favourite plaything, start hiding it around the house, at first in very obvious places where he can seek it out with his eyes, using the word intended to be the command such as 'Seek' or 'Find'. After a while hide the article in more obscure places where the dog has to use a combination of nose and eyes to find it. It is essential that all this is treated as a game using tit-bits, praise and laughter, for serious training comes later.

Teaching the dog to take scent is another part of training to be treated as a separate exercise and should be done when alone with him. Rub onto the hand something that has an appealing smell, such as liver or tripe, then hold the hand out to the dog two inches from his nose, palm towards him, giving the chosen command and the dog will stretch towards the hand and sniff. That dog has now taken scent, so give him whatever it was that he smelt so that he remembers it as a pleasant experience. Keep doing this, lessening the smell on the hand each time, but still rewarding with something tasty. Eventually a freshly washed hand can be offered to the dog and, sure enough, he will take the scent of it. Give plenty of praise and tit-bits and the dog will think 'that's the easiest trick I've learned yet!'

Once the dog has learned to take scent, his toy should be substituted with a piece of knotted rag, which will be perfect for hiding in and under things, and also ideal for wrapping round or tucking into strange articles later. Start with a straight retrieve of the rag, getting the dog used to picking it up. Follow this by playing with it in the same way used when the toy was hidden, to accustom him to identifying it from other articles. Distinguishing his rag from other household objects will not take long, so to progress set up a scent area with a few immovable objects like the coal scuttle, or an upturned flower pot, practising a straight retrieve into them. Once sure that the dog can distinguish his article and is used to working among strange objects, try placing his rag behind a large one so that it is out of sight. The next scent pattern should incorporate one or two items that can be retrieved, such as cardboard folded so that it stands like a tent. At first the rag is put in full vision to leave little room for mistakes, allowing the dog to fetch the article by sight alone. Add a few more retrievable articles, then start hiding the rag under the cardboard tent, so that it is out of sight, but the dog must use his nose to find it as he did when his toy was hidden. Finally any remaining irretrievable articles can be replaced with paper items, or articles such as matchboxes or pieces of hosepipe and one or two cardboard tents, under which the rag can be hidden.

Up until now the exercise has been totally informal without making the dog wait before being sent, or requiring him to sit in the present or finish positions. At the stage now reached the finish is still not used, but the article should be taken at the present. However, the major progression of this exercise is for the dog to take scent before being sent to discriminate, and as he will be using his nose much more, hide the article completely out of sight so that he cannot rely on his vision.

The dog is given scent by placing the hand an inch or two in front of his nose, allowing him to inhale thus taking the scent. A mistake is being made if the dog's nose is smothered with the hand, for not only is it unnecessary, but he may object to his nose being handled in such a way which will have the effect of his concentration being on the hand rather than on the scent of it. It is also difficult for the dog to take scent if his nostrils are closed. Hence we refer to the dog *taking* scent as opposed to being given scent, and there is the world of difference.

Scent discrimination is an exercise that can always be a game which most dogs love playing, so as with all dog training, take time avoiding the temptation to progress too fast. In the Class B scent discrimination test all the articles are the same, such as table mats, hosepipe, knotted rags, rolled newspapers etc. Get the dog used to this new experience by preparing many clean knotted rags, which should be kept in a sealed plastic bag when not in use. These rags are going to be used as blanks, so they must not contain the handler's scent. If someone else can be persuaded to wash them so much the better, but in any case tweezers must be used by the handler to avoid touching them.

At first only place one sterile rag among the Class A pattern until the dog becomes more confident, then one at a time exchange further sterile rags for the Class A articles. By progression all these articles will be replaced by clean knotted rags, with the tweezers being used to ensure that they are not contaminated with the handler's scent. The dog will almost certainly investigate the clean knotted rags, but he should find his own. If he doesn't either progress is too fast for him, in which case revert to Class A scent, or the dog has not been taught to take scent properly. In the latter case forget the actual discrimination and turn the attention to the dog taking scent, until he understands what he is doing. Another alternative is that the article is over scented, thus the handler's scent is flooding the nearby articles. Think of scent like the ripples that are caused by a pebble entering a pool of water, It will give an idea of how confusing it can be for the dog. The larger the pebble the further out the ripples go, and the same applies to the amount of scent put on a rag. The more an article is warmed the further round it the scent spreads.

Once the dog is working the sterile knotted rags and returning with the correct one, help should be enlisted from a stranger to the household to scent rags as decoys. Place just two sterile rags on the ground, asking the decoy person to place theirs amongst them, then the handler's rag should be added to the pattern. By reducing the number of articles the dog is less likely to make a mistake, for when he first smells a decoy and is then unsure, if he is confronted with many other rags from which to make his choice, confusion may prompt him to bring any rag in. If this scent is successful add further sterile blanks, possibly using another additional decoy scented by a different stranger to the house.

Before attempting to try the dog on more difficult Class B scent articles, practise many retrieves with strange objects such as are likely to be used in the Class C retrieve test. The dog must be accustomed to picking up unusual articles so that he can cope with whatever is supplied by a judge. A way of giving the dog more confidence to do so is to wrap his nice old familiar rag around, or tie it to, or tuck it into, whatever he is to retrieve, possibly using an elastic band to hold it in place. He will smell his own scent plus the handler's, and nine times out of ten will pick it up. Then collect several of the same items for practising Class B scent, with the rag attached to the one the dog is to find. Eventually his rag can be dispensed with so that he is working a Class B scent pattern without aids.

Moving on to Class C scent discrimination is nowhere near the problem that it might have been, as the dog's Class A article can be unknotted to be used as a scent cloth. Without using decoys, place the cloth amongst others that are sterile. The dog is already accustomed to collecting his rag, having discriminated between many others and the only difference is the lack of knots, so that he is now being asked to do Class C scent discrimination, but still on his handler's scent.

Teaching the dog to take scent from a cloth handled by a stranger should be taught separately in the same way as he was taught to take scent from the hand, except that a tit-bit should be held behind the cloth which contains the stranger's scent. When the dog has taken scent of the cloth, he is given the tit-bit hidden under it, and eventually he will be taking the scent of the cloth, whether it contains the scent of his handler or that of a stranger. At this point in the training programme sterile cloths are prepared and placed in a plastic bag, or a screw top jar. These are the cloths that are to be used for the handler's scent, which, providing they are prepared by the handler, may be touched. To ensure that the blanks are kept sterile someone else should prepare them, whilst a third bag of cloths to be used as decoys must have similar treatment. To ensure that there is no confusion between the bags or the contents, three different coloured cloths can be used. Two of the unscented cloths should be placed in the area by using the tweezers, these we will refer to as blanks, the handler should then scent two cloths from the other bag, adding one to the pattern. Holding the remaining cloth in the palm of the hand, and allowing the dog to take scent by holding it a fraction away from his nose, he should be sent out to discriminate. If the dog works the cloths and brings the correct one back without trouble, then another blank can be added. When the time comes to introduce decoys again, it is preferable to revert to two blanks and one decoy. Each time the dog is sent to discriminate, two fresh cloths should be used for the handler's scent, and any blanks or decoys that the dog picks up or mouths should be replaced. By doing this it avoids the dog searching for his own scent, as in the showring the judge's cloth will not contain any canine scent. Progress in this way so that eventually the dog is working and retrieving satisfactorily a full Class C scent test including two different decoys.

With many dogs that are taught correctly, scent discrimination can be as simple as the way I have described it, however, the world is not perfect and sometimes there are problems. An inexperienced dog will need to be taught to be familiar with as many different types of material used for Class C scent discrimination as possible. To do so practise retrieves with silk, calico, winceyette, cotton and heavier fabrics such as felt. Cloths containing weights, or with clothes pegs attached, are frequently used by judges, and if the dog has not been familiarised with the uneven weight distribution, it is likely that his pick up will be untidy, with the resulting loss of marks.

There are dogs that pick up each article to check it by taste. Such dogs have formed the habit of taking scent through the mouth as well as the nose, so the handler should revert to Class A scent and, if he picks up his article and then spits it out to check the others, go back to placing the rag amongst one or two irretrievable articles. Always call him in by just the use of his name as soon as he has the correct article in his mouth, thus avoiding him spitting it out. This will also help to speed his return. If he should bring back the wrong article don't reprimand him. Take the one he delivers, then collect the correct one and send him out once more after letting him take scent again.

It must be remembered that if the handler's cloth or article is the furthest away and the wind is blowing strongly towards the starting point, all the cloths are likely to hold a certain amount of the correct scent. Equally, if the decoy is at the back, the dog may pass the correct cloth because it doesn't smell right, and then inevitably he will pick up the decoy as it is the only warm scent he can find. Again be warned against the dangers of over scenting the article and subsequent confusion to the dog.

Never correct the dog in the scent area. If the handler adopts the habit of telling the dog he has the right or wrong article, he will wait for a signal before picking up, or will pick up a cloth and just stand there. He will, in effect, let the handler do scent for him! So don't risk it. If necessary tie the other articles in the scent area to heavy objects, so that if the dog picks up the wrong one the scent area corrects him, not you! Don't say anything at all, just let him try until he finds the right one, then give plenty of praise. This is a useful way of dealing with the lazy dog who will not use his nose, preferring to pick up the first cloth that he finds.

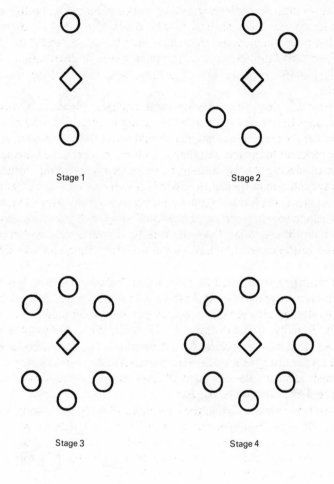

Fig. 6   Scent: Circle pattern training

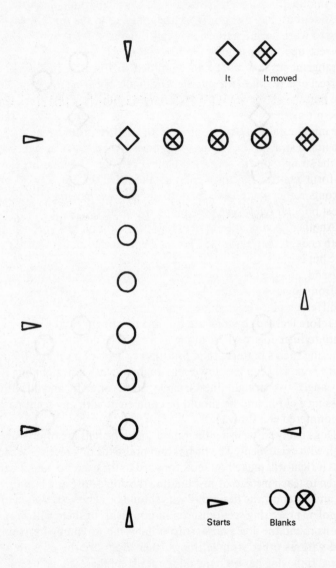

Fig. 7   Scent: Line pattern training

One of the most difficult scent patterns for the dog to work is a circle, with the decoy being part of the circle and the judge's article in the middle. For some reason most dogs will go round and round the outside, but they will not work the middle. So the way to teach the dog to work such a pattern is by putting out three articles, with the correct one in the middle. When the dog is used to working this arrangement, two more can be added to form a square with the correct article still in the middle. Gradually try using more articles in the pattern until eventually it becomes a full circle. At this stage it doesn't matter where the correct one is, the dog will always start in the middle and then try the circle. Other patterns can be taught from the initial straight line. Cloths or articles can be added at right angles to the straight line to form the shape of a letter 'L', or across the top to form a letter 'T'. It is a good idea to teach the dog to work these layouts rather than leave them to chance, as they are amongst the most popular ones to be used in the showring.

Another good practise system is to peg cloths on to a line secured at both ends so that it is taut. The handler's cloth is not attached to the line but is placed on it, with the dog being sent to work the line from one end, and then from the other. Next he can be sent from either side or from angles to the side. To the dog it will appear that the cloth is in a different place each time, when in fact this is not so. He has therefore learned to work the full line thoroughly and to expect the cloth to turn up anywhere along it. Teach the dog to work two lines by using such a pattern, then four in the shape of a square, then six, and so on. The dog has now been taught to work a straight line from any angle, two straight lines, a circle, an 'L' or a 'T', and all without missing a cloth, and he should be competent with any scent pattern encountered at a show.

Dogs really enjoy using their noses, and the tails are often wagging high with excitement. The tit-bits and praise the dog receives when he gets it right will make him look forward to the exercise, and if care is taken to teach instead of just holding the dog's nose and hoping that he understands, the desired results should be achieved. Watch other handlers practising scent discrimination. Half of them will wrap the cloths round the dog's nose, stuff it in his mouth, pump his stomach and various other strange things, their dogs are the ones that fail scent. If the dog has been taught to take scent there should be no need to handle him. Just hold the cloth a few inches from his nose and he will do the rest.

9

The Sendaway

The idea of the sendaway can be taught to a puppy from the age of approximately twelve weeks, without him knowing that it is happening. In an area, such as a room or garage, form the habit of putting him in the down position at the same place all the time, which he will become used to without being aware of the motive. If this is done consistently, the time will come when entering the room that he will pull ahead of his handler, when he should be let off the lead and given the command 'Away' as he runs to his place. The pup will probably not realise that he has been given a command or that he is doing what is required, but subconsciously the word 'Away' will be registered. Painlessly, he has been taught the basic action of going away when hearing the command without any association of displeasure. An additional help is to use an old blanket as part of his bedding, so that when it has acquired his scent, it can be put on his place in the training room. An advantage of this tactic is when later moving the puppy's sendaway place the blanket is moved as well, thus the sense of belonging is transferred from the location of the blanket to the blanket itself. When the dog reaches this stage, he should be pointed to his blanket prior to being sent, and when of his own accord he lays on it, he should be given the command 'Down'. Whilst the immediate down is taught as a separate exercise, this will build an association of the command with the act of going down.

Teaching the dog to look straight is an important part of the sendaway test, as most judges require the handler to stand up straight before sending their dogs. This education can be started by placing him in the present position, facing towards the sendaway area. In such a position the handler has his back to the sendaway area and can cover the dog's eyes before, and whilst turning round. The hands are then opened so that they act as blinkers, with the dog only being able to see straight ahead. Whilst doing this use the command 'Look Straight', before slowly removing the hands. Nine times out of ten the dog will head towards whatever he sees first, which should be the sendaway area. With patience this small aid will be found to be invaluable, as most dogs that go in the wrong direction do so because they have a wrongly preconceived idea of where they will be going, having had a chance to look round the ring first. When standing upright to send the dog, if his head is slightly biased to one side, gently run a finger along the opposite shoulder, which will have the effect of correcting the angle of the head so that it is pointing straight. In competition, prior to sending the dog, although required to stand upright with the hands away from him, when training, practise sending him whilst the hands are still acting as blinkers. This will serve as an additional aid to never letting the dog go wrong.

Obviously setting the dog up straight and sending him away on the first command is all to no avail, if when he reaches the box he runs through it or turns to look at the handler. Therefore the immediate down is a part of training that is essential. The dog will probably already be familiar with the command 'Down' and the foot aid that accompanies it, therefore to start with, putting him down in the heel position at the halt should not present any problems. Develop this to walking at a moderate pace, using all the aids, and when ready, give the command 'Down'. Remember that the command must be instantly obeyed, with the left foot immediately going into the check chain so that the dog goes down. On no account must continual commands be used, nor must the dog be fussed until he complies. After all this is a command with which he is familiar, and therefore it is not altogether forgivable if there is not an immediate response. However, assuming that the dog will go into the down whilst walking at heel when given the command and foot signal, try dispensing with the latter. It is better to drop this aid while he is still close, then it can immediately be brought into operation again if necessary. Once the dog is used to this, loosen the lead and let him walk a little way before giving the command, then join two leads together, which will gain distance but retain control. Once the dog will drop instantly at the end of the lead, let him off and give the command whilst he is still very near.

The distance can be lengthened as his confidence grows, but only when sure that he understands the command, and instantly obeys. The immediate down can now be added to the sendaway whilst still using the training room, and as he has become used to dropping on his blanket of his own accord, the command must now be given before he does so.

A variety of sendaways are used in the showring, of these there are three distinct types with which it is good policy to familiarise the dog. To do this will require the use of three additional sendaway instructions to indicate to the dog where he is going. When using the original sendaway training area, take advantage of the fact that the dog has his place to which he will always go, by using the command 'Get On It'. This will be useful when the judge is using a mat, a piece of carpet, a mark, or a cross on the floor. Next put four posts or bollards round the sendaway place, telling the dog 'Between Them'. Many judges use pegs or four uprights to form a sendaway box, so this will probably be a command frequently used. A third command which will not be used so often is 'Post'. Teach this type of sendaway by putting a post at the back of the sendaway place. These commands should only give the dog an idea of the type of sendaway, as he should not necessarily be sent to a marked place, but sent away in a straight line until commanded to drop.

When watching the sendaway at shows it becomes obvious that some dogs are always practised to the same length at the training club. When required to go a greater distance these dogs lose confidence. To avoid this, try setting up three boxes in a row, one with a piece of carpet in it, one with bollards around it and one with a post by it. First send the dog from one end to any of the boxes so that each time a different box is used, then do the same thing from the other end, thus accustoming him to being sent on short, medium and long sendaways and running through decoy boxes. Also send him over lines and pegs, for sooner or later he will encounter such things at an obedience show, taking all in his stride providing that this part of his sendaway training has not been overlooked.

If the dog hesitates before or during the act of going away, it could be that he lacks confidence, so although not actually teaching him the exercise, call him into the box thus using a Novice recall with a down at the end. Also, if the dog lays with his paws outside the box don't tap them, for when the steward calls 'forward to the box' he will sit up in apprehension of the handler's approach. A much better method of curing the problem is to put a jump board across the front so that

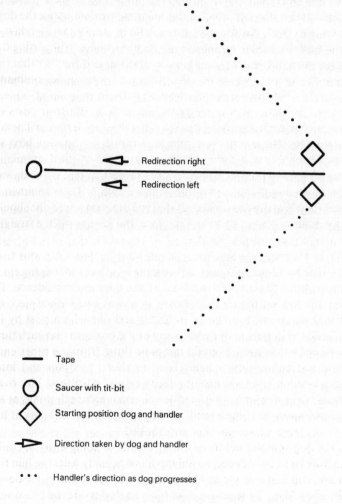

Fig. 8 Redirection

he cannot lay with his paws over the front line of the box. This training can then be taken a step further with boards or stakes placed all round the box to encourage him to curl up inside, in fact the box can be made progressively smaller in this fashion to encourage him to curl up really neatly. Avoid putting a tit-bit in the box as this will only make him sniff, with the result that the immediate down will be lost, which will be reflected in the marks awarded by the judge.

Trying to teach the dog the sendaway by throwing a retrieve article in the box is another erroneous method, for he is just as likely to present the handler with a marker peg at the next show!

It is a good idea to keep the dog to a trot in the sendaway, as most dogs have a bias towards their leader leg when they canter, losing marks in the showring for deviation caused by curving into the box. Tapes are useful for curing a dog that curves, as they funnel him in a straight line without the possibility of the wrong direction being taken.

Whilst aiming for an accurate sendaway the handler might wish to teach the dog redirection. The obedience schedule does not mention redirection, and my own views are that dogs should not be re-directed in the showring, but judges should mark the dog on the basis of the point that dog reaches the first time. However, this is not always done, so I will explain how to teach this exercise, but be careful for a dog easily becomes confused between the sendaway and subsequent redirection.

Set up one straight tape, then with the dog on the lead give the command 'Go Left' prior to walking together along the tape. When reaching the end a tit-bit should be his reward. Whilst this is done repeat the command several times, as it will be a little while before he understands what is required of him. Progress with patience, gradually loosening the lead and moving a little way from the dog, but not until sure that he knows what he is doing should re-direction be tried without the lead. When first attempting lead free don't move far away, and put a tit-bit in a saucer at the end of the tape so that the dog receives a reward without the handler going to him. Once the dog is conversant with this exercise and the handler can direct him at a distance, take him to the other side of the tape teaching him to go right in the same manner, but only try to teach one direction at a time to avoid confusion. The danger with redirection is that the dog may develop the habit of heading out anywhere, and then turning and waiting for the handler to do the thinking for him by giving further directions to the box.

The recall is just the same as was taught for Class A except that it now becomes the final part of the sendaway. However, when training, to avoid anticipation don't always call the dog. Vary the system by sometimes walking straight to the box to praise and release him, and at other times, prior to going to the dog and releasing him, walk in patterns such as might be used for the recall from the sendaway during competition.

The biggest pitfall with the sendaway is always practising the same distance, so remember to vary the boxes and distances without forgetting that it is a three part exercise. Looking straight, sendaway and immediate down. Try not to think because the dog is a little more advanced that he is infallible, incapable of making mistakes or forgetting what he's been told. He can and will. So be patient, don't rush him, remembering the tit-bits and what a clever boy he is!

10

Distance Control and the Advanced Heelwork Positions

Although Distant Control can be taught to a very young pup it may interfere with his Novice Stay exercises, so it is probably best to teach the first stage early then forget about it until the dog is working a good Novice round. Always use the word 'Control' before doing any part of the exercise. The dog will soon learn what it means, for if one movement at a time is practised with a tit-bit as a reward at the end, he will enjoy the exercise. Distant Control is a test where the dog has to lose and gain ground, with the ground lost compensating for forward movement, so that after six positions he is not more than a body length over the point from which he started. It is no good making him afraid of a marker line, as rather than cross it, he will finish up lying sideways on, or miss a position. Instead teach him to move into each position a certain way, bearing in mind that a dog that moves in any direction more than his body length will lose points in competition. The sit gains ground, the down loses ground with the stand being neutral.

THE SIT TO THE DOWN

Start by teaching the sit to the down, perfecting this movement before attempting any others. The dog should be on the lead in the sit position with the handler standing at a right angle close to him. Holding the lead in the right hand so that it loops towards the floor, place the left foot as near to the collar as can be managed, then applying pressure with the foot whilst taking the strain on the lead, give the command 'Down'. This exercise must be practised on its own, teaching the dog to go straight down without shuffling.

However, don't go on until the dog becomes bored, but while practising use tit-bits and profuse praise after each down. Never allow the dog to lay flat on his side, making sure that he goes down with his forelegs straight out in front with his full attention on his handler. Not until the command can be given without a foot signal should progress be made to the next stage.

THE DOWN TO THE SIT

The dog should be on the lead in the down position, with the handler standing at right angles to him. The lead is held in the right hand leaving the left hand free to lift it back behind the dog's head, thus applying pressure to the neck. The right foot slides sideways to the dog's paws to push gently against them while sliding the left hand up the lead and giving the command 'Sit'. It will be found that the aids can gradually be dispensed with by slowly lessening the lead pressure until it becomes unnecessary, then by sliding the right foot towards the dog's paws without touching them. This foot aid is useful when trying the exercise away from the dog, the sight of its movement usually being sufficient to remind him of what he should be doing.

Even when the dog may be capable of both the sit to the down, and the down to the sit without lead assistance, when combining them revert to the starting position using the lead plus the foot aids. Only practise the combination of the two positions once or twice, then break the exercise, praising the dog and giving him a tit-bit. Don't be afraid to take it easy, for the slower and more thorough the progress the more likely are reliable movements. As the dog gains confidence responding to the commands, the lead can be dispensed with whilst the foot signals are retained. Eventually the handler can move away a few feet at first, then when facing him, give the commands using exaggerated foot signals. If the training so far has been thorough, these signals will ensure immediate response from the dog until the command is all that is necessary.

If the dog insists on moving forward when going into the sit, tie him low and tightly, enabling him to lay down comfortably. He will then have to move back into the sit because no forward movement is possible, which is a most important factor. It is not a question of teaching the dog to stay behind a line, but teaching him a series of movements which gain very little ground, or that leave him on the same spot from which he started.

THE SIT TO THE STAND

A step forward into the stand is acceptable so don't worry if the dog makes ground slightly, however remember that the stand should be neutral for forward movement without more than one step being taken. Start with the dog on the lead in the sit position, holding the lead in the right hand while standing at right angles to him. The left hand will act as a funnel to guide the lead back from the dog's neck, while the left foot slides under his tummy lifting him into the stand with the toe. The right foot is placed in front of the dog's paws almost touching them, to discourage forward movement. The command is the dog's name followed by 'Stand' which should be given in a different tone to that used for the sit, therefore avoiding any possible confusion between the two.

If the dog is swinging his bottom away from the foot, stand him next to a wall or a chair, or any similar obstacle that will make sideways movement impossible. The foot aid becomes invaluable when eventually moving away from him, for it can still be used to give the signal in conjunction with the command.

As with all stages of Distant Control training, this one must be perfected on its own, ensuring that the dog is confident before attempting the next movement, or combining it with previous stages.

Dogs rarely wag their tails when standing during this exercise, so the handler must endeavour to make it as pleasurable as possible by the use of praise combined with tit-bits.

THE STAND TO THE SIT

Placing the dog in the stand, adopt the starting position. Holding the lead in the right hand, use the left hand to funnel it back from the dog's neck, applying slight pressure to his front paws with the right foot, simultaneously giving the command 'Sit'. The dog should move his front paws back by one or two paces, which means that from the stand to the sit he will save a little ground, thus compensating for the two paces forward he must take to go down. When he has perfected this under the control of the lead with the foot movement no longer being necessary, try moving away gradually, but reintroduce the foot signal when doing so.

When the dog has mastered the four previous movements, the last two can be taught, which are combinations of what the dog already knows.

THE STAND TO THE DOWN

Use all the aids to start with so that the dog cannot go wrong, it being more difficult to correct mistakes than to get it right in the first place. So having placed the dog on the lead in the stand position, apply the down aids while giving the command 'Down', which should not cause any problems if the sit to the down has been perfected. As with all the other movements dispense with the aids gradually, then re-introduce them as signals when moving away from him.

THE DOWN TO THE STAND

To teach this movement we make use of the dog's name combined with the sit aids to get him to adopt the sit position as the first part of moving into the stand. It will no doubt be remembered that the dog's name should have been used as a request in conjunction with the recall command, so therefore it can be used to start him moving, with the aids ensuring that he does so in the way we want him to.

The handler should stand in the usual starting position with the dog in the down position. Simultaneously the sit aids are applied with the use of his name, immediately followed by the command 'Stand' and the application of the stand aids. There must not be any pause between the name used with the first foot aid and the command combined with the second foot aid, as one fluid movement is required.

Before attempting these foot movements with the dog, it would be advisable to practise them alone, as a certain amount of dexterity is required. However, after a little practise it becomes quite natural to the handler. With the weight of the body taken on the left foot, the right foot slides sideways towards the dog giving the signal used for the down to the sit movement. Immediately this has been accomplished the weight of the body is transferred to the right foot, enabling the left foot to be moved forward and raised to give the sit to the stand signal.

It does no harm to remind the reader once again that as with all Distant Control movements, before attempting to move away from the dog, this one must be perfected beside him by using all the aids. Until he makes the perfect movement by just the use of his name coupled with the command, no attempt should be made to move away, but when doing so re-introduce the foot movements as signals to the dog, until such time as they become unnecessary.

These last two movements must be taught separately, only being combined when the dog has perfected each one at a distance from the handler.

With all Distant Control training, keep it short, spending just a few minutes on each session. Ensure that the dog is always enjoying the exercise by the use of praise, with training always ending on a happy note.

Once the dog knows all the separate commands start combining them, then when moving away, ask someone with whom he is familiar to apply the aids while giving the commands yourself. This ensures that the dog does not go wrong even though some distance away. If the person applying the aids praises the dog the habit of being praised after each stage by his handler will be broken. Remember that the dog must never be allowed to make mistakes, so when trying to move away without help, do so gradually.

It is invariably necessary in the showring to hold a position card, so whilst training hold up a mock card, or even the hand, palm towards the body. It could be that if continually standing with the arms to the side of the body, a movement such as raising a position card might be mistaken for a recall signal.

Practise Distant Control at the training club under distracting conditions, but only when the dog is perfecting the complete exercise at home. At first ask the instructor to shout numbers rather than the positions, so that the dog does not anticipate the words. Next ask him to shout the positions, but when first trying this stand beside the dog so that he has to wait for the handler's command before moving. When the dog really knows the exercise the instructor can shout opposite positions to those which the handler will command him to do. This kind of distraction helps to simulate show conditions where people in other rings may be shouting different instructions. It is very important to have the dog's full attention during this exercise, especially on the first command. Try varying the volume at which the commands are given, two commands loudly, one quietly, then perhaps four loudly followed by two quietly. This will keep the dog's interest, making him pay even closer attention. Think of how necessary it becomes to pay attention to someone who whispers, when conversely there is a great desire to stop listening to a person that shouts incessantly, then apply this logic to dog training. The very thing that we want from the dog at all times is attention, so it really is useless to be the proverbial Englishman who shouts loudly in his native tongue in an endeavour to make a foreigner understand. Also vary the number of positions given, so that the dog is not expecting the standard six. Give two positions, then return to him, then four or one, just keep it unpredictable.

Bearing in mind that there are many kinds of markers or lines in the ring, it is a sensible precaution to familiarise the dog with the various markers used. Once the dog is really confident, put a strip of metal on the ground, or draw a line, but do remember not to reprimand him for moving over the line or make him nervous of crossing it. If he persistently makes ground, then go back to each stage using the lead plus the aids, until he has learned the correct movements.

Never let the dog disobey commands, re-introducing the aids if there is no immediate response. If the dog gets into the habit of repetitive commands it will be necessary to use them in the ring with marks being lost, so ensure that he responds the first time.

If the methods I have described are used with painstaking care the dog will not normally move forward more than his body length, however, if bad habits have been formed there are other aids which might be used to advantage. A piece of string nine inches away from the dog at his chest level will allow him to adopt all three positions whilst containing unnecessary forward movement. A jump board or fireguard have been used for similar purposes in the past, but that nine inches of clearance is important or he will not be able to move at all.

With the emphasis placed on not allowing the dog to become apprehensive of the line, remember that the exercise should always be completed by moving him in a backward direction. Dogs are usually pleased when their handler returns so this method of releasing the dog will not only discourage him from crossing the line by a body length, but there is also little point in teaching the dog to walk completely over the line each time the exercise is finished.

Whilst it is sometimes necessary to return to the dog when he is wrong, it is very important to occasionally return to give him praise and a tit-bit when he is right. By doing so it avoids apprehension of the handler's return. Even if the dog misses a position or takes an incorrect one, don't rush back to correct him but forget the exercise for a while and go on to something else. If he has crossed the line it is fatal to push him back over it, for at the risk of stressing the point too heavily, the dog must not be allowed to become apprehensive of the line. No matter how slowly and carefully the exercise has been taught, if the dog does not like crossing it, he will fail time after time. Remember always praise the dog when he is right, ignoring it when he is wrong, for any apprehension associated with this exercise will result in ring failure or a dog that works under duress.

THE ADVANCED HEELWORK POSITIONS

There is always a danger that if teaching a young dog the advanced heelwork positions too early, he will be made apprehensive of heelwork itself. The signs of this are when the dog slows up tending to work in a crouching manner anticipating the command. So the first rule is do not attempt to introduce positions into the training until the dog is almost ready to be entered for Class C. Obviously the exercise will not present as many problems as it might if the dog is working Distant Control satisfactorily, being familiar with the positions and the commands.

The main difficulty to be encountered is discouraging him from paddling, this being the term used to describe the dog that gradually comes to a stop by taking further paces after the command has been given. A jump board set up where a position is to be given will help to avoid paddling, however, a large portion of success can be attributed to timing and footwork. It does help if to begin with the positions are taught with the dog on the lead, stopping next to him to use all the aids which ensure that he adopts the required position. He is then told to stop still while the handler walks round him, stopping at his side again for the pick-up until he becomes used to it.

When the dog adopts the required position immediately, the circle can be enlarged becoming more of an oval. This move can also be used whilst still stopping next to the dog for both the leave and the pick up. Far better results will be attained if the handler concentrates on one position at a time, not attempting to teach another until the dog has perfected it in a confident manner.

The timing of the commands and the footwork are critical. Always try to give the command at the same time as the left foot comes down, so that as in the basic stay exercises, the dog is left by taking a pace with the right leg first. This should help stabilise him, as the tendency is for the dog to follow the left leg, which of course reflects efficient training!

A few additional aids may be needed to teach the positions, such as a body belt for the stand, which I have found is the best way of teaching this position, it being unnecessary to stop, bend down, handle or fuss the dog. A further advantage is that as an aid it is easier to dispense with than a hand or a foot. For the sit a wand may be the answer, however, do bear in mind the earlier warning that it can cause the dog to swing away, so only try this aid with caution. For the down a gentle push on the withers will probably be a good enough reminder.

Enlarge the circles gradually, for when the handler disappears behind him he may move slightly to get a better view of where his handler is going.

Avoid taking a breath visible to the dog before giving a position command. Once the steward has called 'first position coming' the dog will more than likely tense slightly in anticipation of the command, with a sharp intake of breath from the handler being enough to give away the intention, resulting in the dog taking any position. This breath problem can also arise with the pick up. Do not reprimand the dog in these circumstances, such action will only confuse him as he will think that he has been clever in reading his handler's mind, gaining a preconceived idea of what was wanted. Some dogs are very quick on the pick up, either working forward or jumping up. In these cases use the remedy of turning left immediately on pick up, which will help to cure the problem.

If working Class C only, don't always practise positions with heelwork, more often than not excluding all halts. There is nothing worse than a dog that grovels on his stomach waiting for a position command. This can be overcome to a certain extent by asking someone to call out 'first', 'second' or 'third position coming', without giving the command to the dog so that he learns to ignore the steward. Another possible cure is to enlist someone to call positions whilst the handler gives different commands.

During early training when the dog was taught to sit he will have become accustomed to the hand signal used as part of the three aids. This same signal can be used to advantage as an aid for the advanced heelwork sit position. If insufficient to get the required response, add the Distant Control sit aid of the right foot being drawn towards the dog's front paws.

For the down, a transition from pressing on the dog's withers with the left hand to only giving the command, is continuing the hand movement as a signal without touching him.

Care must be taken with the hands when giving the 'Stand' command for many dogs miss this position because of thoughtless training. For example, if the hands have been used to give signals for the sit or the down, it is foolish to use them for a stand signal as well. Having said that, many handlers successfully use a stand hand signal, but maybe they have trained the other two positions in a different manner to that which I have described, thus avoiding confusion. However, I have suggested that the handler should use a left foot signal to teach the Distant Control stand, therefore it follows that this same signal can be used to advantage with this heelwork position.

During heelwork, without any apparent command or signal from the handler, dogs are often seen to stop to take a position. It is my opinion that this is invariably caused by the handler inadvertently giving a signal without being aware of it.

Experts have stated that dogs cannot reason, but I would ask why in the showring after a dog has been given the first position, he should sometimes decide to take a second without being requested to do so. Surely it is possible that after the first position he is thinking about the other two. In consequence, if two positions are given in close succession followed by a long stretch of position free heelwork, apprehension of the third position can cause the dog to lag or stop.

During training it is not advisable to give the positions in the same place, or very quickly the dog will start anticipating them. Therefore never allow him to get a preconceived idea of when a position is coming, by varying the place in which it is given as much as possible. When the dog can perfect the positions at home and at the training club, ask the help of the instructor to simulate show conditions by calling 'Positions coming *NOW*', and 'Stand', 'Sit' and 'Down' in a loud voice. The handler should ignore all these instructions, either continuing with heelwork or giving the dog opposite positions to those being called. Another dog can be given a retrieve along the side of the hall whilst positions are practised. All these distractions simulate show conditions and will quickly show the benefit of the basic 'watch me' or pay attention lessons. The three heelwork positions need not be difficult if only one is taught at a time in short sessions. The same old rule with a slight difference applies. Never let him take a wrong position or miss one, then he will never know how to. Use tit-bits at the end of each session, always keeping him sufficiently interested to allay any fears of lagging, and if plenty of praise is used, who knows, his tail may even wag when in the stand position.

11

Hearthrug Tips and Training Don'ts

HEARTHRUG TIPS

These Hearthrug tips are designed so that the handler can practise training in confined areas, such as the hall of a house. Just three to four square feet is all that is necessary, and it is quite amazing just how much can be taught to a dog in such a small area.

All initial training must be carried out at home, and only when perfected can it be tried at a training club. The dog learns very little in the environment of the club and it's main purpose must be seen as that of a practise area and a place for training advice. The dog training club is also of great use to accustom the dog to noise, strange people, other dogs and the general hubbub that he would encounter at a show. Every day ten to fifteen minutes should be set aside for training, and if this doesn't seem very long to cover the necessary ground, these Hearthrug Tips will serve as a check list from which one or two exercises at a time can be chosen to concentrate upon. These tips tighten the dog's work so that he is tidy, they also provide opportunity for the handler to improve footwork and the dog's attention. Don't underestimate the short daily sessions. They build a lasting relationship of trust and confidence between handler and dog.

The way to teach all of the following exercises has been described in earlier chapters, but they are outlined separately so that just what can be practised in confined areas is understood.

1. The dog can be taught to sit, and sit still in any position, be it sit at heel or at the present or away from the handler.
2. With the dog on the lead sitting still, practise walking round him keeping the lead slack. If he is only just learning this exercise, don't walk straight round but move away in stages, going back

each time. By building up in this way it will soon be possible to walk straight round without stopping, and without any movement from the dog. This is the start of the sit for the recall and a sit for the stay exercise.

3. With the dog on the lead, practise his recall by either walking backwards and encouraging him, or just flicking the hands towards the groin whilst giving the command.

4. In the confined area the dog can be taught the meaning of the command 'Down' and 'Stand' without moving at all. From this the immediate down can be developed, which should be executed by the dog in the manner that the word immediate describes.

With just four exercises the dog has already been taught the basis of the Novice Recall, the Sit, the Stand, and the Down Stay. All this without even going outdoors.

5. With the dog sitting at heel and the handler taking short paces to the right, he can be taught to close up in the heel position and to sit straight every time, but it is necessary to use the three aids. Eventually the handler will be able to move away to the right by just two inches and the dog will close up.

6. The turns from a stationary position can all be taught as part of Hearthrug Training. Refer back to the chapter on deportment to ensure that the footwork for these turns is understood.

7. The dog can be left sitting while the handler takes one or two paces away, and by flicking the lead and the use of the voice, he can be taught the Class A recall.

8. With the dog sitting at an angle and the handler at the end of the lead, he can be taught to come into the present position with a straight sit every time. How often has that crooked present cost half a mark or more?

9. The dog can be taught to sit still holding the dumb-bell or the retrieve article, either at heel or at the present.

10. Teach the dog to pick up articles from the far side by placing the left foot next to the left side of the dumb-bell.

11. The logical progression from number eight is for the dog to be called into the present position holding the article firmly.

12. Whilst sitting at the present with the article in his mouth, he can also be taught to sit still whilst the handler walks round him and back to the present position before taking it.

13. With the article or dumb-bell in the dog's mouth, recalls at an angle can be practised.

14. Both the conventional right hand, and the left hand finish can be taught. To do so requires very little room for manoeuvre.
15. The start of a sendaway is quite possible in a confined area. By placing a blanket only a yard away, the dog can be taught to go and lie on it.
16. Distant Control is another favourite for Hearthrug Training. The lead, the voice and the footwork should all be used.

So there really is no excuse. Hearthrug Training will only cost a few minutes and a few square feet of space in which so much training can be done.

THE DON'TS

1. *Don't* jerk the lead unless the dog is a mature adult that has developed a lot of bad habits. By the quick turn of the wrist a little short sharp zip of the lead is much better, but a jerk will only cause him to be apprehensive of the lead and the hand movements.
2. *Don't* use the dog's name in the wrong place. His name should only precede a command if he is being called. The use of the name being reserved for the recall, retrieve and practising the return from the scent area. The only exception to this rule being Distant Control.
3. *Don't* forget that if the dog is never allowed to go wrong correction will be unnecessary.
4. *Don't* ever let the dog become bored by over training an exercise.
5. *Don't* allow the dog to become apprehensive of any exercise, but teach carefully without letting him become confused.
6. *Don't* ever correct the dog for a fault, but ignore it and apply the aids next time so that he cannot go wrong.
7. *Don't* lose the temper. If feeling at ill with the world, today is not the day to train and the dog is better left alone.
8. *Don't* move off from a heelwork halt until certain that the dog has completed the sit. Whilst quick sits should be practised, allow a couple of seconds before moving off and so avoid slow sits.
9. *Don't* be afraid of practising two about turns in succession on one spot. Such a move will tighten the dog on this turn.
10. *Don't* bend the body during heelwork, only the arms and legs should move.
11. *Don't* have too loose or too heavy a check chain, it should just fit over the dog's head.

12. *Don't* have too long a lead. 3ft 6ins to 4ft is sufficient. With more it will only get in a tangle.
13. *Don't* have too light a lead if owning a small dog. A heavier lead helps to keep him close.
14. *Don't* be afraid of taking a quick pace out of the heelwork turns particularly when at a slow pace.
15. *Don't* feed the dog immediately prior to competing or training.
16. *Don't* take the dog into the show ring unless he has recently relieved himself.
17. *Don't* take right angle left turns when teaching the fast pace to a young dog. Take a left wheel at first until he understands.
18. *Don't* work bitches in season.
19. *Don't* work one dog in front of another that you own. The dog being worked will not concentrate as he should and the dog watching will be confused, being unable to obey the commands.
20. *Don't* always sit in the same place at class.
21. *Don't* let the dog sit under chairs or hide.
22. *Don't* over praise the dog.
23. *Don't* attempt to train the advanced heelwork positions until the dog is almost ready to be entered in Class C.
24. *Don't* always practise advanced heelwork positions during training.
25. *Don't* forget to play with the dog. Break up training sessions by playing with him therefore making training great fun.
26. *Don't* take any notice of what is written throughout this book if you are successful using other methods.

12

The Obedience Dog Show

Having paid to enter an obedience dog show, probably travelling many miles, it is foolish not to take advantage of anything that might improve the dog's chance of success. Arriving in sufficient time seems quite obvious, but if the journey would normally take two hours additional time must be allowed for unexpected traffic jams, breakdowns, punctures, plus all the other things that can happen on a journey. The handler that arrives just before required to work will not be giving the dog a fair chance. Just as much as the handler needs to relax after a frustrating journey, the dog will also need relaxation plus exercise. Before taking him near the rings it is better to ascertain in which ring the dog will first be worked, and if there is anything about the ring or the test that is likely to give him preconceived ideas, avoid this happening. Assuming that the class has now started and that all is well, the dog can be taken to the ringside to absorb the atmosphere and become accustomed to the steward's voice. This apart, it is wise to allow him to take in the general hubbub that is part and parcel of such events.

Whilst I don't like to memorise a round for fear of anticipating the steward's commands, some handlers do, but much can be learned from looking for possible problems connected with the test. If, within the first few paces of heelwork the judge has set a position, left or left about turn, the handler can be caught napping, completely unready to execute that part of the test in a manner to the dog's advantage. The retrieve article can be ascertained for possible problems, such as throwing a light weight article across the wind direction, which may cause the dog to return at an angle unless the throw takes wind into account. It may be that if bending or folding the article is permissible, to do so would facilitate a clean retrieve, or when offered the article by the steward, only touching it in one predetermined place may encourage the dog to hold it at that point. Perhaps a hunt in the boot of the car might bring to light a similar article which can be used for a practice retrieve. If the class has a dumb-bell retrieve, consider where it is best placed whilst being tested on the other exercises. During the retrieve it can be helpful if the dumb-bell ends have been painted white for if there is a brown patch on the ground or the grass is long, the dog is less likely to lose sight of it after the throw. Many dumb-bells are left behind at a show and a handler is more likely to have his returned if the name has been written on it. Like the lead, it is asking for trouble to leave the dumb-bell on the ground inside the ring, but if the dog is inexperienced, place it at the far side of the table so that he is less likely to be distracted by its scent. There are judges that are very fussy about where the lead is placed while the dog is worked. I like to put it over the right shoulder and clip it under the left arm so that it is worn like a bandoleer. Worn on the body it is handy should I require it quickly, but really it makes no difference where it is placed if the judge objects to it being worn in such a way.

Whilst I am not in favour of galloping my horse before a race, a short practice warm-up can be helpful to most dogs, but beware of over-working him so that he is past his peak when under test. If the dog hasn't perfected the exercise prior to the show, training him on the day is surely too late. Should it be essential to practise the sendaway, keep well away from the ring in which he will be worked for the place selected for the practice may become the one he will go to under test. A quick way of being branded a cheat is to take any action that may unfairly influence the dog to go in the right direction of the sendaway. Believe me, neither judges nor experienced competitors are foolish, being wise to all the time honoured tricks. Good judges are constantly on the look out for malpractice, and fellow competitors are likely to send the offender to Coventry. We all like to win but only if achieved in a fair manner can there be a sense of true satisfaction.

When given a choice of position for the stay tests, many points can be taken into consideration which may help the dog. I once lost an obedience certificate having left my dog sitting on an ants' nest. When I rejoined her at the end of the Down Stay test she was sitting with six ants crawling on her nose, which need never have happened if I had been more careful. Rabbit droppings are something to be avoided if possible, for the dog may have his mind on country chases if left lying amongst them. Take into consideration the weather so that the dog can be left in the most sheltered side of the ring if raining, and in any shade if a hot sunny day. Sometimes one side of the ring is more noisy than others, particularly at a show that includes breed classes, with spectators jostling outside the ropes or ill behaved children swinging them. The ropes that determine the ring have a fascination for young children who seem unable to leave them alone. Leaving the dog next to the entrance to the ring is not good policy. It is the place where people congregate, and should the handlers be leaving the ring to be out of sight of their dogs, it is possible for disturbance to occur in the process.

Stay tests are responsible for many of the show management's problems. Even though the time at which the test will be judged has been well advertised, some competitors seem to arrive late. No doubt we are all guilty at times, it not always being our own fault, but the considerate handler will usually endeavour not to keep the officials or fellow competitors waiting. If a delay is apparent, it is unwise to let the dog settle for too long either in the sit or the down position, the ideal being to position the dog comfortably just before the steward calls 'last commands'. In this way the dog will not be required to keep still for a period well in excess of that required by the rules.

Attending an outdoor dog show in any capacity means being prepared for all the likely changes in the weather. Most essential are a good set of waterproofs and lightweight waterproof boots, but if possible working the dog in light weight shoes or plimsoles will allow the handler to be less clumsy with the feet. I consider a few canine first-aid items kept in the car an insurance against the more common mishaps. If the dog swallows something by mistake soda is a useful remedy for making him sick, hopefully ejecting the offending matter. During the summer months wasps can be a nuisance with dogs snapping at them, sometimes being stung in the process. In such cases vinegar dabbed on the place where the skin has been punctured will help to ease the dog's discomfort.

THE HANDLER AND THE SHOW OFFICIALS

Running a dog show can be a thankless task, and whilst it is not the intention of this chapter to specify how it should be done, competitors can help make the show run smoothly. Once large classes have been split into two or more parts it can mean that the Show Manager is running 14 or 15 classes which is a demanding task. There are rules about the time of arrival and it is most important that they are complied with and enforced if necessary. It is very helpful if the competitor reports to the scoreboard steward of the classes that have been entered, enabling his name to be marked as present. There are those that avoid doing so for fear they may be asked to work their dog, such inaction often meaning that the steward will need to search the showground later to see if they have even arrived. This is most unfair and also rude, as is the competitor who, deciding to take no further part in the class, scratches without advising anyone. These small points of co-operation, although matters of courtesy, are often overlooked when they could help to make life easier for everybody.

Many handlers like to tie their dogs whilst not working them. When doing so, ensure that whatever the lead is affixed to will remain static, taking the weight of the dog should he pull. The knot should be one that cannot be undone by the dog, yet will enable him to be quickly released by the handler. Remember that a dog's teeth make short work of a lead if they wish to free themselves, so consider using a benching chain if this is a problem. The lead or chain should be affixed in such a manner that will enable the dog to lie, sit or stand without becoming entangled, so try tying slightly above the dog's standing height. Do not tell him to stay or adopt any particular position, but rather let him do as he pleases, thus removing the possibility of disobedience. If he is of the noisy variety, it is unfair to leave him near a ring causing considerable annoyance to officials, competitors and spectators.

If leaving the dog in the car, ensure that he has sufficient air, particularly on hot sunny days, and consideration should be given to shading the vehicle by means of sheeting or similar material which must still allow air to circulate. Wherever he is left, water will be a requirement. It is all very well and good chatting about dogs over a cup of coffee, but has consideration been given to the thirst of the dog?

If all these things are taken into account they might just give the dog a chance, so create some good luck of your own; it beats talking about the luck of others.

If the show starts at 9 a.m. the judge will need to arrive much earlier. No doubt there will be old friends to greet, a proferred cup of coffee, a ring to be set up, and stewards finally briefed. All this can mean leaving home as early as four or five a.m. It may be pouring with rain from the time he arrives to the time he leaves, or he may be unable to seek the shade on a sunny day. It is unusual for his reward to be monetary, settling instead for a happy day's dogging. With all this borne in mind, give him a fair crack of the whip by never keeping him waiting, or grumbling about his decisions. The majority of judges are scrupulously fair, doing their best to see all whilst remaining constant in their marking. Remember that a thoughtless remark to a friend overheard by the judge can distract him from his task, and that maybe he was in a better position than you to arrive at his decision. I am not saying that some judges don't deserve the comments they get for there is no way of ensuring their competency on any given day, but on reflection remarks are usually better made in private.

Most judges have to go to great lengths to acquire full sets of retrieve, scent articles or cloths, so try and ensure they are returned to the steward when leaving the ring. It is most annoying to arrive home and find many of them missing. I used to be a great collector of other people's articles, tabulating them so that I could practise with the possible articles during the week preceding that judge's next appointment. I don't really think it fair to the judge, hence I ceased this practice some time ago. I have to admit that I think some judges should be more considerate to competitors. If a dog and handler have had a poor round, one ill-considered remark by the judge can have the effect of sending the competitor away very despondent. It would be far better for the judge to say nothing in such circumstances.

The judge that thinks he is helping by giving the poor competitor his idea of how faults should be corrected can unwittingly cause friction between instructor and pupil. Therefore I would suggest that unless the competitor is desperate to seek the judge's opinion, advice should not be volunteered.

It occurs to me that anyone reading this chapter might think that obedience dog shows are fraught with disaster. Of course in reality this is not so, for obedience competitions would not have grown as popular as they are today if this was the case.

I have enjoyed my years of competition and I like to think that this book will help others to do so. It is impossible to pass on years of experience by book alone, but if your dog handling improves by the saving of just half a point, I shall feel that it has been worthwhile.